Michael Bay |

Contemporary Film Directors

Edited by Justus Nieland and Jennifer Fay

The Contemporary Film Directors series provides concise, well-written introductions to directors from around the world and from every level of the film industry. Its chief aims are to broaden our awareness of important artists, to give serious critical attention to their work, and to illustrate the variety and vitality of contemporary cinema. Contributors to the series include an array of internationally respected critics and academics. Each volume contains an incisive critical commentary, an informative interview with the director, and a detailed filmography.

A list of books in the series appears at the end of this book.

Michael Bay

Lutz Koepnick

UNIVERSITY
OF
ILLINOIS
PRESS
URBANA,
CHICAGO,
AND
SPRINGFIELD

Library of Congress Cataloging-in-Publication Data
Names: Koepnick, Lutz P. (Lutz Peter) author.
Title: Michael Bay / by Lutz Koepnick.
Description: Urbana : University of Illinois Press, 2017. | Series: Contemporary
    film directors | Includes bibliographical references and index. | Includes
    filmography. |
Identifiers: LCCN 2017024538 (print) | LCCN 2017039454 (ebook) | ISBN
    9780252050213 (e-book) | ISBN 9780252041556 (hardcover : alk. paper) | ISBN
    9780252083204 (pbk. : alk. paper)
Subjects: LCSH: Bay, Michael, 1964- —Criticism and interpretation.
Classification: LCC PN1998.3.B386 (ebook) | LCC PN1998.3.B386 K64 2017 (print) |
    DDC 791.4302/33092—dc23
LC record available at https://lccn.loc.gov/2017024538

Contents |

The absence of critical writing on Michael Bay is stunning. Most scholars, even those with considerable investment in the study of the popular, show little patience with Bay's cinema of fast-paced action and excess. Few avoid gestures of deep embarrassment and disdain when caught in the act of watching a Bay film. And yet, while there are many good reasons to feel weary about what Bay has done to moving images ever since the early 1990s, there are at least as many compelling reasons to investigate his cinema of world-making as a sundial of larger historical, political, and aesthetic processes. This book is as much an examination of what drives the films of Michael Bay as it is an effort to probe how one can or should write about Bay in the first place—about a director whose output is so immense in scale and reach that it cannot but question traditional ideas of cinematic directorship.

Instead of tracking Bay's evolution in chronological terms, as a narrative of influence and effect, vision and realization, the six essays that follow illuminate Bay's work in terms of certain thematic clusters, formal interests, cinematic interventions, and ideological agendas. Each approaches Bay's "bigness" as a medium of critical commentary and insight. All of them together hope to discover things in Bay's work that neither passionate fans nor polemical detractors are often able or willing to see. Film studies has a long and valuable tradition of embracing the relative smallness of art and auteur cinema as a hallmark of meaning and creativity. Art cinema's lack of shine, its artisanal character, and its resistance against too much narrative, business, effect, and affect have encouraged critics time and again to explore moving images as vessels of critical reflection. The essays in this book consider the magnitude of Bay's work as an equally, perhaps even more appropriate platform to think with and beyond what cinema has to offer. Their task is to examine Bay's films in terms of timely and untimely questions about the state of contemporary filmmaking, the dynamics of cultural and economic globalization, the temporal politics of neoliberal self-maintenance, and, last but not least, the role of spectators in today's world of ubiquitous image flows. Whether you like his films or not, no filmmaker might matter more than Michael Bay in understanding what cinema is today and where it might be heading from here.

Most of this book was written during the second half of a research sabbatical. I am grateful to Vanderbilt University for granting me time to do what I had once, perhaps naïvely, believed the life of an academic to be all about. I am enormously grateful to Jennifer Fay, Justus Nieland, and Daniel Nasset for encouraging me to tackle Bay in the first place. I embarked on this project right after I had published a book on figurations of slowness in contemporary art and written another one on the role of extended shot durations in twenty-first-century art cinema and screen-based installation art. My initial interest to take on a book on Bay must have appeared, to put it mildly, rather counterintuitive; my credentials to engage with Bay's agitated films rather inadequate. I am particularly thankful for Jen's trust and wisdom—she was dead right to assume that many issues key to my previous work were quite critical to understanding Bay as well. A big thank-you goes finally to Sophia Clark and Kellie Smith, and especially to Kate Schaller. All three have been enormously helpful in researching Bay and preparing this book for publication.

Michael Bay |

Cinema

In Michael Bay's *Bad Boys II* (2003), Detective Marcus Burnett (Martin Lawrence) tries to confiscate a beat-up Chevy to chase a criminal through Miami. His colleague, Mike Lowrey (Will Smith), reprimands Burnett for his unsophisticated choice and insists that he let the car and driver go. Burnett halfheartedly contends that small cars have less of an environmental impact than the stylish vehicles Lowrey typically prefers to drive. But in no time they successfully seize another passing car from a car dealer—a classy Cadillac—and promise its potential buyer, legendary Miami Dolphins quarterback Dan Marino (played by himself), to give the vehicle a rigorous test drive. Which Lowrey, to no one's surprise, will do. And which, quite expectedly, will leave a trail of destruction across Miami and turn the seized automobile into a bullet-pierced ruin of its former splendor.

The film's credits present the owner of the Chevy as "Crappy Car Driver," the adjective likely meant to modify both the rather run-down vehicle and the appearance of its operator, the car's preposterous red stripe as much as the driver's garish shirt and gawky sun hat. The scene's crappy car and its crappy driver are certainly not part of the world navigated by Lowrey and Burnett: a universe of incessant talk and assertive action, stylish gestures and unchecked masculinity. Present within the narrative for no more than ten seconds, the Chevy and its driver enter and exit the screen as if they were extraterrestrial objects. They are marked as foreign, as incommensurable with the logic of the story world, and precisely because of this marking they confirm the extent to which the world inhabited by Lowrey and Burnett, the world of *Bad Boys II*, is one that holds to itself, is designed as a self-enclosed and self-grounding process. Crappy cars threaten the speed and ceaseless movement to which both the detectives as well as the film itself owe their existence. Crappy drivers forsake what it takes to count as a goal-oriented agent, a self-directed player, and hence a proper subject in this particular universe on-screen. They have to go, have to be forced to go, so that the film and its heroes may live and enjoy their existence. Strangely enough, however, as he follows Lowrey's order to take off, it is Crappy Car Driver who calls Burnett a freak instead of being called a freak by the film's protagonists himself (fig. 1). An anomaly, an odd monstrosity at the fringes, freaks are freaks because they betray what the rest of the world defines as normal, regular, and customary. And yet, he who calls the freak a freak can never be sure of not being the freak himself, of finding himself on the sidelines of the ordinary precisely because he assumes the power to identify the borders of the world. To call the freak a freak is to do something for which you require simultaneously to be in and abstract yourself from the world, to be fully immersed in worldly things and perceive them as if they were visible in the form of a picture.

In Michael Bay's breathless filmic worlds, ten seconds tick differently than anywhere else on- and offscreen. And yet, there is little reason to linger on this weird scene at all, to really notice and recall it amid the stream of fast-paced images and sounds, if it weren't for one curious detail: the fact that Crappy Car Driver is played by none other than Michael Bay himself. If cameo performances carve out particular spaces within a narrative to display something of extraordinary value, Bay's presence in *Bad Boys II* is at first puzzling. What we get is—the pun obviously intended by the maker himself—crap instead of a jewel, a moment of pronounced banality instead of choreographed awe. Moreover, if cameo roles are typically pleasurable because they disturb a film's fictional cosmos with a trace of the real, Bay's brief appearance here calls attention as much to the reality of fiction as to the fictionality of the real, the way cinema today holds sway over every aspect of how we think, sense, work, and exist. In naming Burnett (Lawrence?) a freak, Bay—at once authorizing and marking himself as utterly foreign to the world of his protagonists—blurs the very ground allowing anyone to talk of freaks, of being outside of what a given world considers to be normal in the first place. His cameo serves as a bridge to a universe of high-speed attractions, an aperture for viewing obstinate men doing unstoppable things. At the same time, however, as it defines freakishness as the order of all things, it suggests that the worlds on either side of the divide—the surface of the screen—might not be so different after all. You can look at the image and you can be in it. Cinema happens on-screen, but we also live in a world where cinema's images of freaks, speed, style, and astonishing action, cinema's ability to animate our looking and engage our senses, is at the heart of how twenty-first-century society produces its past, present, and future as a whole.

Although Bay can be seen in various of his films—as an uncredited NASA scientist in *Armageddon* (1998), an unfortunate bystander encountering Megatron in *Transformers* (2007), an uncredited truck passenger in *Transformers: Age of Extinction* (2014)—his brief showing in *Bad Boys II* is surely the most momentous. Ten seconds, at once piercing and restitching the very fabrics of cinematic time, of how cinema builds worlds so as to rework the viewer's perception. It is not difficult but rather quite tempting to imagine other, more sustained roles for Bay to be played in his own films. Think, in *Transformers: Age of Extinction*, of Joshua Joyce (expertly played by Stanley Tucci): a cutting-edge scientist and engineer, eager to exploit the potentials of the metal Transformium; a technological wizard who is dedicated not simply to programming matter as if he were God, but—similar to a filmmaker and visual effects specialist—to change anything into anything. Think, in the entire *Transformers* franchise, of the role of Bumblebee,

Figure 1: Crap. *Bad Boys II* (2003) |

a loyal Autobot who understands how to reassemble into a Chevrolet Camaro, yet lacks a voice of his own and therefore samples the sounds of radio broadcasts to communicate with friends and foes alike: a master shapeshifter, equipped—like Bay himself—with impressive talents in creative recycling and innovative mimicry, in productively absorbing a wide range of expressive registers for the sake of affecting his onlookers and companions. Think, finally, of the role of Dr. Bernard Merrick (Sean Bean) in *The Island* (2005), a virtuoso in combining science and art, in assessing the workings of the human soul and in redesigning its operations with the help of elaborate virtual reality machines, in—similar to Bay's efforts as a moving-image maker of music videos and commercials in the early 1990s—massaging minds and emotions with highly captivating audiovisual spectacles.

Michael Bay is a graduate of one of the most prestigious liberal arts colleges in North America, Wesleyan University, and his films are neither known for nor expected to deliver scenes of self-reflexive probing—instants in which his films recognize their own status as filmed entertainment and, like a cameo performance, unveil their methods of producing illusion. Make no mistake, however, about the fact that many of Bay's films quite explicitly refer the viewer to other films and in fact elaborate on cinema's power to modulate affects, shape memories, and elicit desire. The protagonists of *Bad Boys II*, as they repeatedly struggle with the correct lyrics of the theme songs of the original *Bad Boys* (1995), certainly know and let us know that they were at the center of a previous film. When the motley crew of *Armageddon* informs NASA about the fact that Houston may have a problem, they in no uncertain terms situate themselves as action heroes whose thoughts, visions, and postures have been shaped by Hollywood itself, in this case by Ron Howard's *Apollo 13* of 1995.

Of all possible choices, however, no film pronounces greater awareness of cinema's ability to bond emotions and engross perception than *Transformers: Age of Extinction*. Early on, the mechanic and inventor Cade Yeager (Mark Wahlberg) and his not-so-reliable partner, Lucas Flannery (T. J. Miller), enter a dilapidated movie theater in Paris, Texas. In search of junk they could salvage for various experimental projects, they end up finding a semitruck amid the theater's ruins, located at precisely the place once inhabited by the cinema's screen. This seemingly defunct semitruck, as it turns out later, is none other than Autobot Optimus Prime, who has gone into hiding because mischievous humans no longer want to ally themselves with well-meaning machines. Optimus Prime's choice of inner exile is telling: a city known mostly for Wim Wenders's art house film of the early 1980s, in which the city remains a figment of the imagination, a place of longing never to be reached;

Figure 2: Metacinema, Bay style. *Transformers: Age of Extinction* (2014)

and a movie theater whose (actual) derelict interior has been previously explored in Teresa Hubbard and Alexander Birchler's single-channel video installation, *Grand Paris Texas* (2009), as a site where fantasy and reality, the material and the imaginary, past and present witness uncanny interactions (fig. 2). While these references might be lost on many of the film's viewers, it is difficult to resist the urge to spin them into a meta-commentary about the birth of blockbuster franchise cinema from the ashes of European art house sensibilities, and the self-reflexive

Figure 2 (continued): Metacinema, Bay style. Top
and middle, *Grand Paris Texas* (Teresa Hubbard
and Alexander Birchler, 2009); bottom, *Paris,
Texas* (Wim Wenders, 1984)

presentation of Optimus Prime as nothing other but a token—a projection screen—of cinematic fantasy production.

Academic critics used to love such signs of meta-cinematic commentary. Self-reflexive interventions, we once learned in seminars and from
the columns of engaged reviewers, revealed the deceptive operations of
the cinematic apparatus, positioned the spectator as a critical observer, and

rescued the art of cinema from the menace of bad mass culture. None of that, these critics would have been quick to add, can possibly be at play when Bay turns his camera on itself, be it in cameo appearances or in scenes that display their ontological debt to the tricks of cinematographic recording, postproduction, and projection. What they, quite rightly, would point out is this: rather than unsettle the pillars of illusion, spectacle, and emotional identification, in Bay's work cinematic reflexivity and meta-narrative playfulness tend to buttress how each of his films aspires to create self-contained worlds in their own rights. The linguistic mishaps of *Bad Boys II* refer the viewer back to the first installment, not to expose the artifice of the filmic world, but to implicate the audience in the director's efforts of franchise building, one film expanding and reinforcing the world imagined in the other. Frequent references to other action features and their heroes, including Bay's own, stress the hold that cinematic images have on people's imagination in contemporary media-saturated society, on-screen as much as offscreen. The unapologetic recycling of individual images such as airplanes flying overhead in slow motion and at dwarfing proximity, or of certain camera movements such as Bay's signature 360-degree shot spiraling around protagonists as they get up from the ground, props the stylistic unity of Bay's cinematic worlds instead of exposing their porosity. And the placing of individual scenes in traditional theater settings, rather than expressing overt nostalgia for a past of creative auteurs and artful filmmaking, simply exhibits the superiority of Bay's own cinema of special effects, high-octane action, and assertive profit-making. Nothing could be more wrong, we would be encouraged to conclude, than to read Bay's cameos and meta-cinematic moments as signs of what had once defined the stuff of critically esteemed filmmaking: the use of authorial and self-reflexive signatures as a weapon against the mind-numbing spectacles of mainstream entertainment.

Contemporary critics, in often highly polemical terms, see little reason to devote any sustained attention to Bay's directorial work, let alone to find redeeming qualities in his films. Kick-started by work and collaboration with legendary producers Don Simpson and Jerry Bruckheimer, Bay's career is seen as that of a master showman, of a man who is solely about effects and affects and unwilling to provide anything worth critical engagement. Reflecting the lessons from Simpson and Bruckheimer, Bay's films are encountered as products that have no qualm about showing up front what critics might want to expose as ideology through fine-grained analysis in more demanding works. Press reviews of new Bay releases typically read like something forced upon the critic and written with considerable resistance and disdain. In fact it is difficult to think of any filmmaker working today whose meta-critic ratings on internet platforms such as IMDb (Internet Movie Database) deviate as widely from his popular user ratings as Bay's, his aggregate meta-scores typically staying way beyond the 50 percent mark—in other words, in regions close to what may easily count as a critical failure or unwatchable bomb.

The laments of well-known reviewers are familiar and fairly consistent, Bay and his films being the bad objects that wear on their sleeves everything that could possibly be wrong with blockbuster filmmaking. For example, Manohla Dargis wrote in her review of *13 Hours: The Secret Soldiers of Benghazi* (2016) for the *New York Times* that Bay "makes big, bludgeoning movies stuffed with nonsense, special effects and military fetishism, and while they are ridiculous they can be absurdly entertaining when they're not boring you out of your mind."[1] Far less forgiving, Roger Ebert called *Armageddon* "an assault on the eyes, the ears, the brain, common sense and the human desire to be entertained. No matter what they're charging to get in, it's worth more to get out."[2] And even though with his next film, *Pearl Harbor* (2001), Bay seemed to shift mode and genre, Ebert has shown as little patience with the final product as he did and has done when Bay exploits science fiction settings to legitimize his hyperkinetic style: "Its centerpiece is 40 minutes of redundant special effects, surrounded by a love story of stunning banality. The film has been directed without grace, vision, or originality, and although you may walk out quoting lines of dialog, it will not be because you admire them."[3] To complete the troika of established film criticism, we should add the voice of Peter Travers, whose *Rolling Stone* review of *Bad Boys II* called the film "the cinematic equivalent of toxic waste" and then summarized: "*Bad Boys II* has everything. Everything loud, dumb, violent, sexist, racist, misogynistic and homophobic that producer Jerry Bruckheimer and director Michael Bay can think of puking up onscreen."[4] Easily the most reviled American filmmaker of the twenty-first century, Bay and his films cause many a critic to doubt the nature and mission of their very profession. And yet, as Dargis's, Ebert's, and Travers's repeated lamentations indicate, Bay's films have also come to serve as fixtures that critics reliably love to hate—events that summon a welcome sharpening and entertaining wielding of verbal weapons.

Michael Bay's relation to moving-image culture resembles that of Donald J. Trump to the political establishment during and after his 2016 electoral campaign. Critics may challenge the narrative incoherence, visual overload, and psychological triviality of Bay's films, only to see the director shrug off their arguments and declare them as failing to understand the central ambition of his work. Reviewers may point out that his films return viewers to boyish and misogynist fantasies, only to be rebuked as brainy nerds who are unwilling to comprehend the visceral pleasures that cinema has to offer. Commentators may consider each of Bay's films as a complete waste of resource, talent, and spectatorial attention, only to hear Bay argue that box office numbers and revenues would prove them utterly wrong. An unrelenting populist, Bay—like Trump—has no quarrel in allowing numbers, statistics, and naked profits to speak for quality and content. For him, Excel sheets tracking global audience records and release returns invalidate whatever critics may say in print about the aesthetic quality of his work. And when it comes to numbers, clearly no other contemporary director has continuously managed to generate as remarkable outcomes and to trump other directors with as imposing financial figures as Michael Bay.

Consider just a few of his successes. The worldwide gross receipts for the first four *Transformers* films equaled around $4 billion, the latter two films of the franchise in 2011 and 2014 cashing in around $1.1 billion each and *Transformers: Age of Extinction* being the first American film earning more money in China than in America or anywhere else and exceeding the GDP of at least seventeen nations worldwide. Bay's net worth has been estimated at $430 million, his annual salary at $65 million in 2011 and $160 million in 2012, making him one of the top earners in the film industry. Whereas his films of the 1990s and early 2000s typically opened on two thousand to three thousand screens, each of the *Transformers* films enjoyed domestic releases to more than four thousand screens at once. The average shot length of his features are among the shortest in the film industry (two to three seconds), while the duration of his films has taken on ever more epic proportions, thus resulting in films whose sheer number of shots necessitates financial investments and workforces far in excess of films made by many others. Although such figures are difficult to tally, cast and crew members in the last two *Transformers* productions easily spiked well into the range of the two thousands, the majority of employees working in visual and special effects studios in various continents. Though considered by Bay himself the weakest entry of the series, the theatrical release of *Transformers: Revenge of the Fallen* (2009) was seen by almost 60 million viewers—a fifth of the entire US population—an astonishing number no doubt due to the fact that, in contrast to Bay's *Bad Boys* franchise and *The Rock*, the *Transformers* series was deliberately designed with younger viewers in mind and, in spite of its sustained violence on-screen, able to receive a PG-13 rating.

No matter how you turn it, any "A Michael Bay Film" today is part of a global business and brand that puts to work thousands of people during the production process and systematically commercializes the pleasure and perception of massive audience numbers for years to come. "People have a hard time believing I'd ever want to do a small movie, but I would love to do something funny and quirky," Michael Bay pronounced early in his career in 1998. "I'm a huge Coen brothers fan. But good small-movie scripts are hard to come by. Maybe if I could get through all these space-shuttle scripts I'm constantly being sent, I could do something really different."[5] That time has certainly not arrived, "small" being perhaps the last word now associated with how Bay builds expansive cinematic worlds and does not shy away—much to the chagrin of his many critics—from allowing numbers to validate their success, the sustainability of his approach to contemporary filmmaking. Although no concrete figures are available, the size of Bay's carbon footprint—how the production, distribution, and reception of his films drain natural resources and impact environmental relationships—certainly figures as second to none.[6]

Turn it as you wish: size essentially matters to what viewers over the last decades have come to experience as "A Michael Bay Film," with Bay's tremendous investments in cast, crew, filming technology, visual and other special effects, postproduction, marketing, and waste production at once echoing and reinforcing the epic scale of what can be seen on-screen. Transformers cry for the big, not the small; stylish cops like Mike Lowrey require screens that do not limit the speed, the spectacle, the thrust of high-powered cars chasing other cars. For viewers and critics alike, for fans as much as detractors, matters of scale—a film's temporal and spatial proportions, its intensity of action, its sense of unstoppable movement, its enormous footprint—serve as unquestionable markers of recognition. You instantly know whether you are in the face of a Michael Bay film when you see, sense, and hear it. Big, loud, and always amid ongoing states of emergency, Bay's films offer universes whose formal organization, stylistic signatures, physical elements, and psychological dynamics are instantly identifiable as being of the same kind—as parallel, albeit entirely self-sustained, worlds made of similar and highly intelligible elements. And yet, whether located in the past, present, or future, these worlds are not mere collections of things, of elements that can be counted or not, that are known or unknown. What holds each and all of them together instead is their underlying drive toward magnitude and epic reach itself, a kind of energy that sweeps across things minute and delicate, has no patience for the humble and intricate, and propels whatever may become perceptible and tangible.

"A world is only a world for those who inhabit it," writes Jean-Luc Nancy, "an ethos, a *habitus* and an inhabiting: it is what holds to itself and in itself, following to its proper mode."[7] What makes Bay's films instantly recognizable is not simply the visual or acoustical presence of fast cars, giant robots, muscular men, and scantily dressed women. It is the unremitting ethos of scale, size, and intensity that dynamizes the overall workings of all his films. It is the underlying impulse to create worlds that are strange, dangerous, and unknown yet seemingly complete and utterly inclusive, so complete that Bay's heroes never show any doubt about dwelling in these worlds, nor do Bay's viewers ever have any chance not to inhabit them, whether we like the logic that holds them together or not. Bay's worlds may be the last that viewers and critics really want to exchange for those that await them outside the auditorium. But the most striking trademark of Bay's work as a director is no doubt his ability to effectively design everything it takes for viewers to encounter screen images as portals to imaginary realms that, on the one hand, have Bay written all over them, while on the other, and in spite of their often violent inhospitality and excess, they present themselves to view as void of any possible alternative.

"World-making" has come to serve as a key word of contemporary criticism for understanding how the architecture of individual works of art echo the developments of contemporary convergence culture and economic globalization. In *Concepts of Film Theory*, Dudley Andrews wrote in 1984, "Worlds are comprehensive systems which comprise all elements that fit together within the same horizon, including elements that are before our eyes in the foreground of experience, and those which sit vaguely on the horizon forming a background. These elements consist of objects, feelings, associations, and ideas in a grand mix so rich that only the term 'world' seems large enough to encompass it." He then added:

> We step into a Dickens novel and quickly learn the type of elements that belong there. The plot may surprise us with its happenings, but every happening must seem possible in that world because all the actions, characters, thoughts and feelings come from the same overall source. That source, the world of Dickens, is obviously larger than the particular rendition of it which we call *Oliver Twist*. It includes versions we call *David Copperfield* and *The Pickwick Papers* too. In fact, it is larger than the sum of novels Dickens wrote, existing as a set of paradigms, a global source from which he could draw.[8]

Bay is no Dickens, nor do his Sam Witwickys, Cade Yeagers, Mike Lowreys, Harry Stampers, and Stanley Goodspeeds produce echoes in the viewer's imagination and memory that are comparable to those of a *David Copperfield* or *Oliver Twist*. Bay's imaginary worlds, however, are of equal depths and extension, resting on a rich array of elements both conscious and unconscious, visible and invisible, that beg the viewer to enter the image and inhabit the world in and vastly beyond the frame. They are rich in texture and detail, so plentifully packed and layered that many viewers miss visible features—whether they belong to the pro-filmic or owe their existence to digital effects—during first-time seeing. They boast with what Eric Hayot calls "amplitude": the distribution of attention to any given object across the spread of the entire narrative.[9]

Each shot in Bay's films is typically stacked with considerable data and information, directing our focus on elements of narrative importance as much as on things that serve no clear purpose except atmospheric or stylistic ones. Though Bay's camera even within individual scenes often seems to jump erratically and in overt violation of classical protocols of editing and continuity, the dynamism of his cinematography nevertheless excels in presenting diegetic spaces as unquestionably connected, so continuous that we have no doubt that these spaces vastly exceed the

Figure 3: Planetary cinema. Top to bottom:
Armageddon (1998); *Pearl Harbor* (2001);
Transformers: Dark of the Moon (2011)

realms pictured during the time of narrative action. Strange beings and unfathomable events may populate Bay's cinematic worlds, reminding us of the limitations of human-centered perspectives in order to understand the sensory field. But whatever we hear and see, conjecture and presuppose, all seems to come—in Andrews's words—from the same source and is part of a suggestive system much larger than the mere

Figure 3 (continued): Planetary cinema. Top to bottom: *Bad Boys II* (2003); *Transformers* (2007); *Transformers: Age of Extinction* (2014)

narrative we encounter on-screen. It therefore is no coincidence that at least half of Bay's films contain shots of planet Earth taken from outer space and that they showcase meteors, spaceships, or communication satellites against the backdrop of our planet or parts thereof. Nearly all of Bay's films involve natural, man-made, or machine-triggered threats to large portions or the entirety of the human habitat (fig. 3). Bay's cinema is a cinema of planetary proportions, of terrestrial urgency. Its narratives, time and again, threaten to destroy the worlds this cinema so effectively conjures for the viewer. Yet in toying with the fragility of human affairs and the challenges of planetary survival, this cinema at the same time affirms its very power to invent and populate—like the novels of Dickens—global horizons of experience, its power to generate a comprehensive sense of worldliness.

When Andrews wrote about the world-making of cinema, the Hollywood blockbuster had just entered the stage. Franchise filmmaking in the twenty-first century asks for certain adjustments of his concept of the cinematic world—in particular, regarding how the worlds and narratives of cinematic fiction today stretch across multiple media and entertainment platforms. The world-building of Bay's cinema, especially his *Transformers* series, is a potent example of what Henry Jenkins has identified as transmedia storytelling: a process in which elements of fiction are systematically dispersed across different delivery channels, each channel ideally contributing another aspect and amplitude to the imaginary world constructed as such. Bay's worlds consist of not simply what we see and what remains hidden on the theatrical screen, but they also feed on and into a whole array of graphic novels, toy production lines, video games, fan websites, music videos, YouTube postings, and so on. They expand into and incorporate what is known and enjoyed in other formats so as to build a narrative conglomerate that would have been unthinkable in the early years of the Hollywood blockbuster. Transmedia stories, writes Jenkins, as if seeking to theorize the imperial footprint of Bay's cinema, "are based not on individual characters or specific plots but complex fictional worlds which can sustain multiple interrelated characters and their stories. This process of world-building encourages an encyclopedic impulse in both readers and writers. We are drawn to master what can be known about a world which always expands beyond your grasp. This is a very different pleasure than we associate with the closure found in most classically constructed narrative, where we expect to leave the theatre knowing everything that is required to make sense of a particular story."[10]

Although many film critics typically celebrate the moment when the final credits set them free to exit a Michael Bay film, what they tend to forget is the extent to which Bay's cinema of transmedia storytelling indeed rebounds with encyclopedic impulses, a collective dispersal of information and knowledge that stretches these films far beyond the site and time of screening. Neither individual narratives nor actual characters of Bay's cinema ever exist in the singular. Each individual Autobot and Decepticon in Bay's *Transformers* films comes with and energizes the making of Wikipedia entries whose length, detail, and complexity easily match entries on grand systematic philosophers such as Kant or Hegel. Such a diffusion of story elements across different media channels expands potential markets for the product as much as it invites viewers to take on different roles and responsibilities in moving the story forward, to fill in possible gaps and make up additional contents. Once simply seen as something to be witnessed on-screen, cinematic world-building thus takes on vastly increased dimensions. It is an integral part of how moving images today are being anchored in and animated by the very fabric of the everyday, lodged into the expanded horizons of what not only children playing with Hasbro toys would call "real."

Until not so long ago, the concept of world cinema primarily belonged to filmmakers, critics, scholars, and institutional contexts invested in the promotion of films that were categorically different from the fare we have come to associate with Hollywood.[11] Often rooted in national idioms, traditions, and styles, world cinema—like world music—was to feature the universal language of filmmaking in all of its cultural particularity and of filmmaking for global audiences. It often involved small, deliberately unspectacular, and artisanal films; relied on so-called art house theaters, dedicated late-night television screenings, and international film festivals for circulation; and largely advocated cinematic products galvanized by the signatures of individual authors seeking control over all significant elements of the filmmaking process. The "world" in and of world cinema was a world that was normatively pitted against popular cinema's reach for global markets. Its lack of shine challenged the culture industry's efforts to standardize pleasure and erase diversity, and its praise of authorship recalled postwar auteurism with the aim of bringing art back to the business of filmmaking, of mobilizing the aesthetic as a medium of difference and diversity against the homogenizing force of profit-oriented film production, distribution, and consumption.

Michael Bay's sumptuous efforts at world-making, within each of his films and across different media platforms, position him as a director producing the very bad objects that advocates of world and art cinema once stridently combated. In their eyes, the bigness of his work does everything to moving-image culture that sponsors of world cinema hope to overturn. Nevertheless, given how Bay's transmedia storytelling, immersive special effects, and narratives of ceaseless activity and self-management go hand in hand with production processes that span different continents, labor markets, media channels, and production units, there are many good reasons to think of this cinema as perhaps the most forceful expression of world cinema today, perhaps the truest exemplar of what it means to design moving images for and in the world under the conditions of twenty-first-century media capitalism. In the eyes of German film critic Siegfried Kracauer, the famous, high-kicking Tiller Girls of the 1920s simultaneously expressed the precarious state of the human body in Taylorist modernity and provided a focal point for transformative energies; as a mass ornament, they at once encoded the rationalist spirit of the time and aesthetically transcended it.[12] Bay's automated organic robots are the Tiller Girls of the twenty-first century. They allegorize the workings of contemporary techno-capitalism as much as they circulate utopian energies that may succeed it. They focalize in aesthetic terms, as objects of sensory experience, what culture in the age of globalization is all about while at the same time surreptitiously embodying a logic that may lead our own present into a different future. No one who is serious about understanding the work of cinema today, of trying to map out the contested contours of world cinema, can afford to ignore the films of Michael Bay.

Cinema is no longer what it used to be when movie theaters monopolized the display of moving images, theatrical exhibition solely informed how critics theorized the impact of motion pictures on the viewer, and to praise world cinema was to praise the art of iconic auteurs controlling each and every aspect of a film's making and meaning. Like the transmedial narratives of Michael Bay, cinema in the twenty-first century exists in the plural. It comes in all shapes and sizes, involves ever more diverse media platforms, and is being consumed in often highly unpredictable viewing situations, at times on the move and in mid-stride, at others in the bright daylight of ambient multiscreen environments, in the enveloping darkness of surround-sound auditoriums, amid the cave-like space of a museum gallery, or in the face of the interactive screens of video games. Though some critics sport the term "post-cinematic" to describe its contemporary condition, cinema is still well among us, albeit in radically expanded and multiplied form beyond its classical existence in darkened theaters. As film historian Francesco Casetti, with admiring open-mindedness, describes cinema's situation today:

> On the one hand, it [cinema] acquires an attenuated character that allows it to insinuate itself in the crevices of our social world: It becomes lighter, more accessible, attainable, and polymorphous, and yet remains part of its own history. On the other hand, cinema redefines its identity: it asks us to accept the transformations it has undergone, and even to project them back in time into its history; only in this way can we establish a bridge between past and present that guarantees that we are in fact still dealing with cinema. In short, cinema's persistence is based on greater flexibility on the one hand, and a sort of continuous self-reinvention on the other, which is entrusted to us and which allows us to recognize what we have before us as cinema and as the "same" cinema, despite all its modifications. Lightness and reinvention: If cinema is to remain among us, these are the conditions that allow it to do so.[13]

Ebert, Travers, and company have many good reasons to think of Michael Bay as a director whose pyrotechnic spectacles extinguish what cinema was once all about. For them, as for many others, Bay's work offers signs not of cinema's persistence or expansion under the conditions of 24/7 screen culture, but of cinema's death, its evaporation, its utter sell-out. Rather than attenuate cinema's weight to recalibrate its distribution, critics typically discuss Bay's films as mindless betrayals of cinema's pasts and futures, as—in Bay's own terms—crap jamming the circuits of cinematic tradition and renewal. This introduction and the essays that follow will draw a different picture of Michael Bay's cinema of global mayhem, excess, speed, and world-making. In spite of its epic narratives and high production values, Bay's cinema is a cinema of lightness. As no one is likely to disagree, it is light because it deliberately refrains from intellectual weight lifting. But more importantly, it is light because Bay's films actively register and participate in the reinvention of cinema in the age of polymorphous and ubiquitous screen culture—that is, outside of the normative frameworks inspired by the viewing conditions of classical cinema.

Once a battle cry of the 1960s avant-garde to challenge both the cerebral elitism of postwar art cinema and the commercial canonization of modernist art, the concept of "expanded cinema" has largely lost its critical sting today and come to describe the ordinary existence of moving images in 24/7 media culture.[14] Michael Bay's cinema offers no less than a key to understanding the fate of cinema after cinema, the afterlife of cinema in the aftermath of its unfettered expansion into each and every fissure of the everyday. It offers a sundial to assess the prospects and memories of cinema in the twenty-first century, including the unexpected transformation of avant-garde hopes into global capitalism's most valuable currency. Not at all shy about what might be crappy about it, the lightness of Michael Bay's cinema nevertheless asks tough questions about what remains of, and what we will recognize as, cinema once viewers happily accede to consume moving images in bright daylight, at all times, and in all places. It visibly responds to conditions that have replaced the sovereign gaze of the singular classic spectator with incomplete, fractured, mobile, and common practices of viewing; in so doing it is of unique value to shed light on how film shapes, and is being shaped by, globalized economies and politics of attention. Far from simply seeking to represent, please, or educate the crowd, the fictional worlds of Michael Bay visualize nothing less than the future of a cinema whose methods of perceptual management understand how to articulate the crowd in space and time itself.

Contrary to temptation, however, we would be utterly mistaken to label Michael Bay an "auteur of action": a reincarnation of the darling of twentieth-century film; a John Ford, Howard Hawks, Alfred Hitchcock, or Fritz Lang of our image-saturated times. Instead, Bay's films document the extent to which the radical expansion of cinema in the digital age has altered the very nature of what it means to create a film, and of how critics may read for possible signatures of authorship. Given the magnitude of Bay's world-making, the size and spread of operations that no single maker could ever claim to control, know, and author in full, three other concepts come to mind to describe the meaning of "A Michael Bay Film," of how Bay's version of world cinema engages new parameters of aesthetic creativity, control, and collaboration. These concepts at first may appear counterintuitive to designate what audiences and critics alike expect from the role of a film director, past or present. And yet, in all of its efforts to build all-embracing worlds on- and off-screen, Bay's cinema of transmedial storytelling clearly requires us to probe new approaches to questions of authorship in order to account for the unprecedented number of wills, talents, skills, visions, techniques, and technologies that animate what we associate with a Michael Bay film in the first place.

The first two concepts are that of the assemblage and the swarm, both typically understood to describe dynamic groupings of diverse elements and processes that are so complex in nature that traditional ideas of agency, of intentional design, of causation and effect no longer hold: the blackout of a power grid, a hurricane, what we have come to call the war on terror. As political theorist Jane Bennett explains:

> Assemblages are living, throbbing confederations that are able to function despite the persistent presence of energies that confound them from within. They have uneven topographies, because some of the points at which the various affects and bodies cross paths are more heavily trafficked than others, and so power is not distributed equally across its surface. Assemblages are not governed by any central head: no one materiality or type of material has sufficient competence to determine consistently the trajectory or impact of the group. The effects generated by an assemblage are, rather, emergent properties, emergent in that their ability to make something happen . . . is distinct from the sum of the vital force of each materiality considered alone. Each member and proto-member of the assemblage has a certain vital force, but there is also an effectivity proper to the grouping as such: an agency of the assemblage.[15]

In press statements and celebrity interviews, Michael Bay prefers to present himself as a strong-willed director and savvy entrepreneur who is able to forge all aspects of individual projects into one unified consumer product. Actor Ben Affleck once did not hesitate to call Bay an auteur in the true sense of the word, uncompromising in his efforts to imprint his creative vision onto each moment of the filmic product, its making as much as its reception.[16] The concept of the assemblage and the related one of the swarm—a moving body of elements forged into dynamic unity "not according to their innate, morphological essences but as expressions of certain movements, sensations, and interactions with their environments"[17]—invite us to turn such statements on their head and thereby do justice to the complexity of Bay's mode of transmedia storytelling and cinematic world-building. Rather than seeing Bay's films as the outcome of a single director's will and intention, these concepts encourage us to approach the filmic worlds of Michael Bay like emergent properties whose movements cannot be entirely predicted or ever be concluded. Like assemblages and swarms, these worlds reveal the force of what Bennett calls "distributive agency": they rely on a mosaic of efforts, movements, talents, and trajectories. And instead of actualizing one initial concept and vision, their shapes at once produce and are produced by the very brand people call "A Michael Bay Film." Bay's worlds are not a distant God's creation from scratch. They are vibrant force fields producing and projecting god-like images of the director to reduce and explain (away) their complexity. But as we know from both Marx and Nietzsche already, it is after God's death—the demise of unrestrained creators—that worldly matters and social affairs become most interesting. Understood as assemblages and swarms, Bay's cinematic worlds—like few others— throw into sharp relief the economic, political, and aesthetic dynamics that govern our globalized existence in the twenty-first century. Though populated with various afterimages of the divine, the magnitude of these worlds' distribution and confederation of agency, in very rare ways indeed, illuminates the contemporary logic of lives, times, and cinemas structured by the power of networks, nodes, and ceaseless, albeit mostly non-transparent, connectivity.

According to *Variety*'s Scott Foundas, Michael Bay is a filmmaker invested in "visceral, big-toy filmmaking,"[18] whose uncompromising enthusiasm for the huge, loud, immense, and encompassing brings to mind another concept—our third—that is able to move the study of individual filmmakers into the era of post-representation mega-blockbuster cinema. Initially coined to speak about entities whose vast spatial or temporal dimensions unhinge traditional understandings of the identity of an object, Timothy Morton's concept of "hyperobject" provides a promising lens to read Michael Bay's efforts of world-making. The term "hyperobject," Morton writes, is meant to

> refer to things that are massively distributed in time and space relative to humans. A hyperobject could be a black hole. A hyperobject could be the Lago Agrio oil field in Ecuador, or the Florida Everglades. A hyperobject could be the biosphere, or the Solar System. A hyperobject could be the sum total of all the nuclear materials on Earth; or just the plutonium, or the uranium. A hyperobject could be the very long-lasting product of direct human manufacture, such as Styrofoam or plastic bags, or the sum of all the whirring machinery of capitalism."[19]

Too big to be conceived or conceptualized, the existence of hyperobjects defies any attempt to develop a metalanguage, a critical outside from which to envision the entity in question. Unlike events or objects once associated with the sublime, the magnitude of hyperobjects no longer promises any kind of experience of transcendence: they do not make us recognize our own smallness, our vulnerability, or our pain as a pleasurable source of human identity. Instead, hyperobjects urge humans to think of history as no longer entirely a human project. Whether they have destructive potential or not, they open our eyes and senses to the agency of entities other than human, and they cause us to envision the world, in all of its immanence and amid all the Anthropocene era's ever increasing disasters, from a nonhuman perspective.

Bay's films themselves are populated by hyperobjects of the destructive kind. They abound with things too large in space and time to be fully fathomed or navigated by human protagonists. Think only of the epic war between Autobots and Decepticons in the *Transformers* franchise; the threat of planetary extinction in *Armageddon*; the aftermath of the Arab Spring in *13 Hours*. As we will see later, the true challenge of these films is not that they entertain the possibility of imminent ends of the world, but that in doing so they recognize that the world as we know it— the world entirely centered on human intentions and perceptions—has come to an end already. For now let us simply face the possibility that Michael Bay's project of world cinema itself, the comprehensive effort in world-making we call "A Michael Bay Film," is just such a hyperobject as well. It is too big in production value to be encountered with traditional concepts of authorship and creative control; its reception spins off in too many directions to be tracked with any existing matrix of audience studies; its blurring of the lines between the representational and the presentational, between work and world, between image and immersion is too complete to allow us to look at this from a position of distant exteriority. Many critics are rightly tempted to see and dismiss Michael Bay as a director of imposing gestures and neo-imperial ambitions. In truth, however, perhaps his most important contribution to the history of cinema is to ask viewers to envision how cinema—its history, its aesthetics, its economics and politics—might look if we abandoned the idea that it was entirely a human project. A project made by humans for humans. A pliable machine simply grafting human needs onto the world.

Assemblage, swarm, hyperobject. Although these concepts are rather unfamiliar to the study of filmmaking, they offer useful perspectives to approach Bay's cinema of unapologetic magnitude—that is, the transformation of world cinema from a cinema of good objects, of deliberate smallness and diversity, to one in which we inhabit and are being surrounded by moving images at all times, everywhere. Assemblages have no windows, swarms no portals, hyperobjects no thresholds or doors. We cannot really enter them. We are always already in or among them. Understood as entities whose size exceeds our ability to think of (film) history as exclusively a human affair, Michael Bay's worlds are ours and all around us long before we know it—whether we like it or not, whether we think of it as crap or not. It is time to allow these worlds to speak to us, to go traveling in and across them, to traverse their environments and map out their topographies in greater detail.

Action

What allows Michael Bay to put images into action and make them act on the viewer is not difficult to identify. Cinematic action and agitation in Bay's films rests first and foremost on highly mobile camera work. Whether "real" or "virtual," his camera is always on the move. Eschewing conventional expectations for establishing shots and visual contextualization, Bay's shots typically commence with moving the viewer directly into a particular setting, at times following the motion of certain objects, at others deliberately running across or against them. Not only do we always find ourselves already in the midst of things, but what constitutes a thing or event in Bay's world typically entails multiple trajectories, relies on motional paths that remain unresolved, and produces dynamic force fields that deny easy acts of spatial mapping and orientation. Second, Bay's visual compositions are energized not simply by frequent changes of focal length and perspectival depth, of areas of sharpness and zones of blur, but by tableau-like takes in which action takes place on multiple planes and layers at once. Typically, the use of zoom lenses helps Bay to stack the image along horizontal axes, allowing unrelated objects, scales, and volumes to co-inhabit the perceptual field and create dramatic tensions that are unknown to the operations of organic vision. Though often void of narrative motivation, this layering of different planes of movement—

recall, for instance, the frequent image of airplanes flying over signs and bodies at terrifying proximity—contracts space and in doing so galvanizes the viewer's perception. Third, ever since his first feature films, Bay's cinematography has heavily relied on camera perspectives that are so shaky in nature that even viewers who are able to halt the flow of images find it difficult to say what they see in the first place. Rack zooms, sudden cutaways, rickety camera operations, bipolar lens lengths, and canted angles charge the image with kinetic energy and position the camera not as a neutral observer but as an active participant in the action. Fourth, while Bay's ever increasing use of visual effects impresses the viewer with things unseen and vistas unimaginable, his often frantic editing maneuvers, pulsating cutting strategies, and elliptical presentation of on-screen action undercut the very exultation produced by seeing the unseen. Editing in Bay's hands serves as a highly calculated method to make viewers oscillate between feelings of visual awe and of haptic assault. It causes us never to rest, never to pause and stay with what we see on-screen, and instead to be shoved and propelled by each new image. And fifth, but by no means least, Bay's musical soundtracks, as they weave themselves into the sounds of action on-screen, create dynamic atmospheres in which stable auditory points of view seem utterly impossible. Especially when engaging the full spectrum of sound mixing associated with Dolby 7.1, Bay's films offer dense soundscapes whose complex movements and kinetic energies are no less effective than those acting on the viewer's eye.

Scholars have debated whether Bay's cinema, in its attempt to agitate the viewer, continues or breaks with Hollywood's classic regime of continuity, understood as a system of creating seemingly seamless impressions of space and time. Although some observers are quite critical of Bay's methods of seizing the viewer's attention at the cost of creating readable images of action—"The rapid cutting, constant camera movement, and dramatic music and sound effects must labor to generate an excitement that is not primed by the concrete event taking place before the lens"[20]—David Bordwell, for one, considers Bay's agitated images and sounds not as a radical departure from but as an intensification of classical continuity. No matter how choppy and freewheeling Bay's camera work may be, nearly all scenes delivered in his and comparable action films of the last decades develop options that had emerged already in the 1910s and 1920s.[21] On the other hand, to counter Bordwell's formal-

Figure 4: Images in action. *Bad Boys I* (1995) |

ist approach as much as the lament of critics such as Matthias Stork,[22] who denounce Bay's images as incoherent, chaotic, and illegible, Bruce Isaacs has argued that once we approach it from the perspective of the viewer, Bay's cinema inscribes a "sophisticated, complexly and deeply affecting mechanics of spatio-temporal continuity" after all.[23]

Figure 4 (continued): Images in action.
The Rock (1996)

While it is true that Bay's images, as they are deployed for visceral effects, often disorient the spectator, fragment the visible field, and offer unmotivated framings of action, his films as a whole recast continuity as a category that belongs to the viewer rather than the film itself. According to Isaacs, spectators are more than able to endow with continuity and coherence what Bay's mise-en-scène, cinematography, and editing may present as fragmented. As a result, Bay "strategically negotiates an aesthetic style founded upon rapid camera moves and restless, unstable camerawork with the elemental desire of the spectator of Hollywood's mainstream action cinema for spatio-temporal, narrative and existential continuity—what I am calling global Hollywood's projection of wholeness."[24] In reckoning with the viewer's drive to recompose the visible and create experiences of wholeness at the level of perception, Bay's films seek to energize the very act of watching contemporary cinema. Rather than simply assault the viewer's senses, his recasting of continuity intensifies cinema's ability to mobilize the senses. It wants to activate the viewer by allowing films to act on us, to appear to us as if they were endowed with their own agency.

Hungarian philosopher and critic Georg Lukács wrote in 1913 that cinema invites us to forget the demands of high art and instead cultivate the naïve and irresponsible aspects of our modern existence: "The *child* in every individual is set free and becomes lord of the psyche of the spectator."[25] Difficult as it may be to imagine Michael Bay reading the work of the grand Hungarian Marxist, Bay certainly has no qualms about presenting his films as vehicles appealing to the inner child in both their makers and their viewers. His pyrotechnic spectacles; his images of robotic toys gaining real-life existence; his narratives of global danger, rescue, and redemption; and, most of all, his presentation of both men and cinematic images in continuous action—all quite frankly aspire to free cinema from taxing expectations and enable the spectator to tap into the unfettered playfulness of childhood. It is certainly tempting to read Bay's appeal to the child in every individual as symptomatic of what action cinema in the age of digital oversaturation for many is all about: a mechanism that is simultaneously catering to, producing, and capitalizing on individual attention deficit disorders—our inability to sustain concentration over extended periods of time without the incentives of spectacle, thrill, seduction, and perceptual violence. It is at least as tempting, however, to consider Bay's efforts to animate images at all costs as an effort to charge moving images with a certain kind of agency in their own right. For Bay, to engage the playful and childlike in this sense would be to make viewers feel what it might mean to face media objects that—somewhat magically—cast their gaze at their viewers and envelop them without their doing. It is also to thus indicate the very need of moving beyond seasoned concepts of spectatorship such as absorption, concentration, and distraction—that is to say, concepts that continue to think of attention from the vista of the traditional humanist subject rather than in light of today's economy of ubiquitous 24/7 flows of mediated images and sounds.

I will have more to say later about how Bay's cinema of action and playful mayhem recalibrates attentional economies of the present, envisioning a viewer that is no longer the viewer of twentieth-century film culture, art, and theory. For now the focus is on the question of what makes Bay's action heroes themselves tick, of what drives their quests and interventions, of how they define and stick to their missions, and of whether and how they grow as subjects when acting in their worlds. Once we have found some answers to these questions, we return to the larger issue at stake here: to what extent the commitment of Bay's heroes to certain activities—their unconditional attentiveness to goal-oriented action—provides models for what Bay's viewers are meant to do with his films themselves, and how this may change what we define as viewership today. Traditional Western ideas of action and attention saw both as key aspects of what it meant to become and be a person. Both expressed our ability to imprint our will onto the world and onto our perception thereof. Both needed and enforced each other to enable the subject to gain control over the amorphous powers of nature and in the process to realize itself as an individual and articulate the shapes of culture, society, and history. Bay's cinema creates worlds that break with this conception. It untangles the traditional relation of action and attention as much as it reconfigures what we traditionally expected from each of these two to do in the first place.

It is important to remember, writes philosopher Rowland Stout, that "actions do not have existence independently of their agents."[26] Action requires actors who intend what they do and interpret it as such. To understand action is to understand what it means for an agent to act. It is to illuminate what it means for someone to act intentionally, to define certain goals and select appropriate means to achieve them. Bay's films are littered with characters—antiheroes, as it were—who are unable to do this; they neither know what they really want, nor do they actually know what they are doing. Following a well-known populist trope, Bay's nonheroes typically are government bureaucrats who are eager to map abstract thought or political exigencies onto the demands of particular situations; military or police officers who, due to their higher rank, appear alienated from the physical challenges and mental flexibility necessary to parry states of emergency; or people whose exorbitant wealth situates them as individuals who simply want something for the sake of wanting and have lost the mental capacity to reflect on their needs or those of others. In *13 Hours: The Secret Soldiers of Benghazi*, the CIA station chief, simply known as Bob (David Costabile), represents the first type: a man of memos, enclosed spaces, remote strategy, and fearful irresolution, who asks his team to "stand down" at precisely the moment when the narrative requires determined action to fend off the Arab enemy. Joe Pantoliano's role as Captain Howard in both *Bad Boys* films and, even more so, Marg Helgenberger's as Miami Police Department superior in the first of the two embody the second paradigm: officers of rank more concerned with proper protocol, with regulations and reputations, than with what it might take to address urgent problems. Though brutally victimized by the film's deranged bodybuilders, Victor Kershaw (Tony Shalhoub) in *Pain & Gain* (2013) exemplifies the third type: a man of considerable wealth whose singular concern with strategic success and monetary accumulation—marked by the film's anti-Semitic rhetoric as a Jewish trait—positions him as deeply emasculated, a mere receptacle of other people's actions, a nonactor truly deserving his victimhood.

A Jew like Kershaw (and Bay himself), Franz Kafka's heroes faced structures inhibiting action without ever understanding their causes and genealogies. They ran afoul of what in Bay's cinema has turned into a league of nonactors, who are progressively unable to pursue their intentions and be clear about their own goals. In Kafka's world a hero's failure to achieve something, his running up against illegible decrees and oppressive bureaucratic arrangements, is often translated into radical disorientation and self-doubt. Time and again, Kafka's heroes rationalize their failure as effected by a lack of focus; they internalize structural power by reading personal predicaments as products of a willful slacking of attention, a brief yet unforgiving absence of intentionality. As if trying to prove Kafka wrong, Bay's perhaps most striking heroes—Lowery and Burnett from the *Bad Boys* franchise, Goodspeed and Mason from *The Rock*, Stamper and Frost from *Armageddon*, Witwicky and Yeager from the *Transformers* series—always triumph over structures that inhibit action. They neither know of metaphysical disorientation, nor do they despair in the face of bureaucrats, policies, and protocols demanding conformity. On the contrary, an essential aspect of what qualifies them as heroes is their ability to sustain action in spite of various mechanisms trying to slow them down, and to maintain a sense of focus, of attention, regardless of the fact that existing dynamics of power cause all kinds of distractions. They could not be further away from the dilemma of Kafka's heroes, action *and* attention being fully on their side, their unrelenting drive toward survival, rescue, and success eclipsing any possibility of self-doubt, of questioning the thrust of intentional action.

Unlike Kafka's sadly insular protagonists, Bay's heroes never simply pursue a cause on their own. Nor do they ever really operate for their own good, no matter how calculating they may be in approaching their respective tasks. Instead, Bay's heroes, often against their own initial will or better knowledge, consistently find themselves in situations that ask them to ignore self-interest; forget about personal goals and allegiances; functionalize their adamant narcissism, self-centeredness, and stubborn egotism for ongoing acts of sacrifice; and in so doing rescue many lives unknown to them, at times even the future of the entire planet Earth. Although once in action endowed with unquestionable agency and perseverance, Bay's heroes typically react to something initially not of their concern. Introduced as prickly individualists, uncomfortable mavericks, or unreserved hedonists, they usually enter the narrative as somewhat reluctant heroes in need of being coaxed into action. Their business is not revenge of prior harm or injustice done to them, nor is it to actively redeem themselves from former mistakes and failures. Instead, what turns Bay's protagonists into heroes are unexpected challenges and emergencies—a literal "calling"—that causes them to overcome themselves, their obstinacy and absorbed ordinariness, and to carry out what appears unquestionably right and legitimate in order to save what requires saving.

Rarely do we encounter Bay's heroes as being haunted by repressed histories to be at once revealed and cleared away in the course of sacrificial action. They always reside firmly in the present and have few outspoken commitments to pressing pasts and futures. They may act in the name of family bonds yet are often shown as members of rather defunct, truncated, unsteady, or curiously absent familial situations. What most of them share is experiencing action as a space to project themselves in new ways into the lives of others. Though we initially might find them at the fringes of society—oil drilling platforms in the ocean, remote farms in Tennessee or Texas, secluded laboratory spaces, high-security prisons—action offers them a medium to connect to the social as steadfast contemporaries. Action, for them, is a way to discover and embrace the present as a crucible of futurity, as a site we need to inhabit in order to ensure that there will be a future at all. Bay's heroes may not always be in a position to spell out the meaning of national belonging, but almost all of them are quick to refer to the idea of the national, its symbols, and its military arms of enforcement as essential custodians of collectivity, of relating to, sacrificing oneself for, and receiving grace from the other.

Though muscular action and naïve gung-ho American patriotism go hand in hand in Bay's films, it is noteworthy that *Pearl Harbor*'s Japanese pilots, as they prepare for their deadly strike in the early morning hours of December 7, 1941, are displayed not as sneaky cowards and evil fanatics, as might be expected, but as patriotic warriors who are as legitimately eager to sacrifice their lives for their nation as their American opponents. Their gaze is fierce and deeply concentrated, their posture resolute and committed, their whole appearance austere and unwavering—all of this not because ideological exigencies have manipulated their minds and engineered useful emotions, but because in the camera's perspective, they are readying themselves to act in the name of a cause larger than their own. True patriotism in Bay's films legitimizes action and focalizes attention regardless of the national body to which it ties the individual.

And let's not fake surprise about this: not one of Michael Bay's films centers on a female lead or allows a woman to assume the same kind of heroic qualities and agential dynamics reserved for their male counterparts. Slight exceptions confirm the norm (fig. 5). Bay's early and later video commercials for Victoria's Secret are all about female bodies, yet no further commentary is needed to imagine how these bodies are captured by the camera's gaze. *Bad Boys I* and *Bad Boys II* sport more assertive female characters, Téa Leoni in the first installment, Gabrielle Union in the second. But in spite of their physical contribution to action and narrative, in the end they largely require the assertive interventions

Figure 5: Unlikely heroes. From top: *Pearl Harbor* (2001); *Bad Boys II* (2003); *Transformers* (2007)

of men to channel their energy most effectively or be redeemed from overwhelming evil. Last but not least, after playing self-assured Mikaela Banes in the first two films of the *Transformers* franchise, Megan Fox was pulled from later sequels because she challenged Bay's directorial persona in public interviews in 2009 and compared his machismo to that of historical despots whom neither Bay nor producer Steven Spielberg were willing to accept as points of comparison. In 2009 Fox said the following about Bay in *Wonderland Magazine*: "He's like Napoleon and he wants to create this insane, infamous mad-man reputation. He wants to be like Hitler on his sets, and he is. So he's a nightmare to work for but when you get him away from set, and he's not in director mode, I kind of really enjoy his personality because he's so awkward, so hopelessly awkward. He has no social skills at all. And it's endearing to watch him. He's vulnerable and fragile in real life and then on set he's a tyrant."[27] Though Hollywood gossip has it that actress and director smoothed out their relation later again, Fox's muscular words got her instantly removed from the project. In Bay's world as much as in Hollywood in general, defiant combativeness in word and deed remains a male prerogative, a subject that will be addressed later in this book.

If Kafka's heroes waver between fight and flight as they focus their attention on the intensity of attention itself, Bay's heroes typically flee into fight, the sustained intensity of required action seemingly eclipsing the very possibility of worrying too much about one's level of necessary focus. And yet, some of Bay's heroes clearly reveal recurring concentration problems during the course of action, a troubling failure to imprint full control over their intentions, perceptions, and mental activities—or so it may seem, at least at first. Consider the protagonists of both *Bad Boys* features, detectives Mike Lowrey and Marcus Burnett. Key scenes in both films show the two engaged in excessive verbal exchanges with each other while finding themselves in life-threatening situations that require determined deeds rather than meandrous dialogue: (1) in the opening of *Bad Boys I* when both detectives get in the middle of a scam trying to rob Lowrey of his Porsche, and (2) in the opening of *Bad Boys II* when both argue over this and that while being surrounded by Ku Klux Klan members who are ready to end the detectives' lives on the spot. Add to this that the latter sequence precedes numerous later scenes in the film in which Lowrey calls on Burnett to pay proper attention to ongoing tasks at hand, Burnett drifts into a mental nowhere land after accidentally consuming Ecstasy, Lowrey himself fails to remember the words of the film's signature title song, and both undergo therapy to work through possible traumatization on the job as much as in childhood. But in both situations mentioned above, Lowrey and Burnett intuitively understand how to jointly switch gear at exactly the right moment so as to make bullets rather than words speak and to overcome their enemies with swift determination. As if verbal bickering, far from merely suspending necessary action, were part of a highly calculated choreography of engagement. As if their focused attention on one would not preclude the possibility of attending to the exigencies of other matter as well. As if concentration and awareness for them had less to do with addressing one distinct issue at a time and more with sensing the dynamic ebbs and flows of an entire situation or environment. As if they—like fish in a school—were true experts in synchronically adjusting their behavior without pause, glitch, and oral coordination to new directions.

What at first in Bay's films may thus look like a moment of distraction threatening possible action actually turns out to adhere to a different model of attentiveness altogether, one in which individual attention has less to do with how a given subject attends to events or images considered in front of and separate from him than with how this individual understands how to be within events and images and go with their flow, how to shape and be shaped by their resonances. Similar to the majority of Bay's protagonists across all of his films, Lowrey and Burnett excel in what psychologist Mihaly Csikszentmihalyi once called the "optimal experience of flow," a way of experiencing skillful activities in play, art, ritual, work, or sports as if they were utterly intuitive and effortless. To experience flow, or what Hans-Ulrich Gumbrecht describes in comparable terms as to be "in the zone,"[28] relies on the

> sense that one's skills are adequate to cope with the challenges at hand, in a goal-directed, rule-bound action system that provides clear clues as to how well one is performing. Concentration is so intense that there is no attention left over to think about anything irrelevant, or to worry about problems. Self-consciousness disappears, and the sense of time becomes distorted. An activity that produces such experiences is so gratifying that people are willing to do it for its own sake, with little concern for what they will get out of it, even when it is difficult, or dangerous.[29]

Once in action, Bay's heroes are enormously good at what they are doing. Their skills in handling weapons are superb; their agility in physical combat extraordinary; their maneuvering of fast-moving vehicles first-rate (with the arguable exception of Burnett). Moreover, rarely do we see them hesitate in their effort to develop viable tactics and strategies to respond to pressing problems. They always know what to do next even if a film's narrative does not entirely clarify how they acquired this knowledge. Self-conscious wavering is as little a need or option for them as facing empty pockets of time or lingering through periods of boredom or ennui. Bay's heroes are always on, at all times and in all possible places. Experts at what they are asked to do, most of them have no attention left for anything not pertaining to their task. Due to their impressive skill sets, they experience their tasks as something best accomplished if not seen as a task anyway. No matter how calculated their activities and interventions might be, they appear unintentional and reflex-like, gracefully (as eighteenth-century philosophers would have argued) integrating the sensory and the cognitive, kinesis and knowledge. As masters of flow, of absorbing skill into intuition, Bay's heroes typically see no reason to question their tasks and missions as they go along. For them, to know what to do and to rely on their ability to do it suspends any further need to doubt possible goals. Whatever flows carries its own moral legitimacy and authority. What you do for its own sake, and without conscious subjectivity, does not tolerate distrust and skepticism. Nor does it need narrative to back its cause. Flow in Bay's films instead is autotelic: it generates its goals, its thrust, its values, its normativity out of itself.

Three exceptions to Bay's mapping of action as flow deserve to be named, each of them temporarily throwing into question the autonomy of flow-like action, and yet all of them in the end enlisting words, narrative, and discourse in the service of intensifying effortless attention and agency.

Case One: The path of Stanley Goodspeed (Nicolas Cage) to determined action in *The Rock* (fig. 6). The film tells the story of a rogue US general—Francis X. Hummel (Ed Harris)—who takes eighty-one tourists hostage on Alcatraz and directs stolen warheads at the city of San Francisco in protest against the government's handling of veterans benefits. A geeky FBI biochemist in Washington, D.C., Goodspeed is sent to help resolve the situation. He is ordered to team up with a group of military specialists and an imprisoned British intelligence agent, John Patrick Mason (Sean Connery)—a proven expert in breaking out of Alcatraz—to take over the former jail and defuse the weapons. Aside

Figure 6: Finding flow I: Stanley Goodspeed
(Nicolas Cage) in *The Rock* (1996)

from his scientific knowledge, Goodspeed has little to qualify him for this mission. He is a man of the laboratory, not the field. Although he is good at dealing with bombs in contained environments, he certainly lacks what it takes to navigate the contingencies of the world. He loves to drink, play the guitar, and generally live a life of low commitment. When his girlfriend informs him in the opening sequence about her pregnancy, Goodspeed's reaction, at least initially, is less than adequate. Once on his mission, his physical symptoms of fear serve as comic relief as much as a counterpoint to Mason's ferocious masculinity, the latter not really aware of Goodspeed's professional status in normal life. Goodspeed's loquaciousness at once compensates for and renders audible what his highly competent military team members perceive as a critical deficit, possibly endangering the entire mission. Nothing about Goodspeed, as he embarks on the undertaking, radiates flow. He is self-conscious about his lack of skills. His narcissism and curated subjectivity get in the way of becoming an integrated member of the squad. He is a specialist, but his specialism is initially not coupled to or absorbed into a regime of bodily movement and action. Even when having entered the bowels of the former prison, Goodspeed cannot help but to question the mission itself. Repeatedly we see him pushed to the edges of the frame. His head turns nervously, his body twirls with visible unease, while Mason, on the other hand, appears calm and centered, so calm amid the storm he can even crack jokes about Goodspeed's unheroic demeanor.

The tide changes, and Goodspeed begins to emerge as a hero of flow and optimal experience: after General Hummel's men surprise and kill the entire squad of military intruders, Mason and Goodspeed find themselves as the last remaining operational units, Mason threatens to leave the island and abandon the mission, and Goodspeed begs Mason to stay and continue the task, revealing his true identity—his not being a tactical field agent or a James Bond—to the former spy. Critical to Goodspeed's transformation is, first, his displaying his FBI identity card to indicate that he is not exactly qualified for the kind of military intervention expected from him; and, second, Goodspeed's using his primary talent—the use of words—to outline the full danger of the situation, including the threat posed to both Mason's daughter and Goodspeed's girlfriend, both located in San Francisco. Although it will take Mason a few more instants to return fully to the mission, for Goodspeed the moment of coming out, of deploying words, signs, and gestures to validate his position and the limits of his abilities, opens up the decisive portal toward resolute action. Henceforth, we will see Goodspeed not only effectively and with utter concentration doing what needs to be done but also doing it as if no thought, reflection, explicit intention, or pausing calculation were necessary to carry it out. Normally presented as the enemy of swift action, words here unlock the possibility for Goodspeed to get into the zone. They unfasten the brakes of self-consciousness and allow the action-averse scientist to become fully absorbed into the challenges ahead of him and save the lives of millions of Bay Area residents.

Case Two: Lincoln Six Echo (Ewan McGregor) vs. Tom Lincoln (Ewan McGregor) in *The Island* (fig. 7). The only Bay film thus far that flopped at the box office, *The Island* is a dystopian science fiction film that transports the viewer into a future of human cloning, genetic bondage, and brutal organ harvesting. Lincoln Six Echo is at the center of what, by the end of the film, amounts to a revolt of the cloned slaves against their biological masters—people who sponsor and engineer mindless biological duplicates to capitalize on human dreams of eternal life. Lincoln Six Echo's memories and dreams are implanted, his emotions flat and indiscriminate. He is programmed to behave like an obedient child, surveyed at all possible times for possible glitches, may start to develop autonomous cognitive energies, but would never pass the threshold of any given college admission process. He doesn't know how to drink or how to enjoy drinking. Nor how to kiss, let alone make love. He has excellent motor skills, yet when he maneuvers challenging physical situations within—and after his breakout, outside—the hi-tech organ farm, there remains something deeply robotic about his movements. All things told, Lincoln Six Echo gives bad press to academic scholars' more recent embrace of post-humanism. Rather than free the human from the confines of traditional concepts of identity and subjectivity, he enters the film as a profoundly shrunken subject, a person without soul and identity, a body with reduced or enslaved consciousness who is unable to endow his life with reflexive and ethically complex forms of agency. He acts as if remotely controlled, notwithstanding the fact that he will run up against the system that not only produced him but also uses a vast array of immersive entertainment technologies to warrant his conformity. If Stanley Goodspeed starts out as having too much

Figure 7: Finding flow II: Lincoln Six Echo (Ewan McGregor) and Tom Lincoln (Ewan McGregor) in *The Island* (2005)

consciousness to enter the optimal experience of flow, Lincoln Six Echo begins with too little and, ignorant about his being—nonbeing?—as a genetic slave, lacks what it takes to gain experience in the first place.

Though he is initially unable to articulate his own expectations, in the second half of the film we follow Lincoln Six Echo, together with fellow escapee Jordan Two Delta (Scarlett Johansson), to Los Angeles to track down Lincoln Six Echo's biological template, sponsor, and titleholder, Tom Lincoln, a wealthy Scottish experimental designer. When Lincoln Six Echo realizes that his memories are nothing but engineered duplicates of Tom's, and as a result gains full insight into the operations of the cloning institute, in a sudden show of wit, cleverness, and dexterity, he manages to pose as Tom, have private military contractors kill Tom, and then stage a formidable upheaval at the cloning institute that leads to its physical destruction and the release of thousands of genetic slaves. The decisive transformation of Lincoln Six Echo takes place after a prolonged car chase inside the ruins of a former church. The chain of events develops roughly like this: Tom holds his gun to Lincoln Six Echo's head; the institute's chief mercenary, Albert Laurent (Djimon Hounsou), tries to figure out who is who; Tom, with his Scottish accent, claims to be the original and only Lincoln Six Echo; Lincoln Six Echo, after a moment of pensive pause and with a controlled British accent, claims to be Tom; Lincoln Six Echo cunningly attaches his ID wristband to Tom's arm; Tom gets ever more hysterical about not being taken for a clone, whereas Lincoln Six Echo gains ever greater confidence and cool in faking not being a technological reproduction; and Laurent's gun alternately targets either of the two, finally fires at the real Tom, and thereby promotes Lincoln Six Echo to what he was designed merely to copy.

It is not entirely clear whether Laurent at this point already sees through Lincoln's plot or not. Introduced as a contractor from Burkina Faso, he will later support Lincoln Six Echo's slave revolt, mapping the fight against colonialism and genetic cloning onto each other. What matters more, however, is how Lincoln Six Echo in this triangulated shootout scene assumes the power not simply of language and linguistic sophistication but of playacting and performativity to trick Tom at his own game and claim agency over his body. "I am Tom": the very speech act through which Lincoln Six Echo usurps Tom's identity situates him as a being who is capable of identity to begin with. It endows him with what will characterize his persona throughout the rest of the film—namely, the kind of concentrated action and attention, the flow-like execution of skillful activities, represented by the majority of Bay's action heroes. To stand up in word and deed against his master allows the slave to recognize himself as slave, free himself from bondage, and develop the very self-consciousness that experiences of flow need to suspend in order to achieve optimal results. Hegel could not have been happier about how Bay, in the ruins of theological certainties, stages the conflict between sponsor and clone as a struggle to the death—a dialectic in which the master becomes enslaved by his slave's labor and the former's loss of self, identity, and life goes hand in hand with the latter's assumption of agency and unwavering resolution.[30]

Case Three: Optimus Prime (voice: Peter Cullen), coming out of retirement in *Transformers: Age of Extinction*. After defeating Megatron's troops in the epic battle of Chicago during the previous installment of the franchise, the Autobots had to go into hiding because government forces began to recognize all Transformers as potential security threats and decided to develop their own versions. Although once considered invaluable aids in humanity's efforts to fight destructive Decepticons, all remaining Autobots now find themselves hounded by the government, marked for extinction. If Optimus Prime, in earlier and later installments, typically brackets the films' narratives with grand speeches about human-machine collaborations and heroic sacrifices, in *Transformers: Age of Extinction* it takes nearly thirty minutes to hear his voice and see his robotic gestalt enter the film. Saturated with numerous painful moans and groans, his first words, spoken to Cade Yeager (Mark Wahlberg) as he repairs Optimus Prime's dilapidated truck shell, are far from friendly: "I'll kill you" (fig. 8). It is only after Yeager, like a caring nurse, explains to Optimus Prime his ailing physical condition, indicating that he wants to help the robot in the safe environment of his home, that Optimus Prime calms his frenzy and starts to trust the idiosyncratic inventor. "Cade," he exclaims before declaring his identity and then collapsing weakly one more time to the ground, "I am in your debt. My name is Optimus Prime. My Autobots: they are in danger. I need to go." More repairs, more sessions of gaining mutual trust, more exchanges about bad government politics and human reliance on Autobot aid are necessary in order to enable Optimus Prime to do so, to restore his full powers, transform the Transformer into an operative leader and fighting machine, and reenlist him for the fight against the Decepticons, against their plan to extinguish life on Earth in a way that is similar to how they extinguished—as recalled in the opening sequence—prehistoric dinosaurs.

Transformers are exemplars of seemingly unfettered becoming and self-help, symbiotic shapeshifters who reconstitute even if we often are unable to tell exactly how the parts of one shape metamorphose into that of another. It's so difficult to terminate them because they understand how to reorganize their parts swiftly, work around certain deficiencies, and, when fully functioning, are all about flow. Their cognitive abilities are not in the way of their motility; their "bodies" integrate mechanic and organic elements so effectively around given tasks that nothing else seems to matter and they appear to be doing what they are doing for its own sake. In *Transformers: Age of Extinction*, Optimus Prime has initially lost his power of becoming, an ability that defines him as Transformer to begin with. A mechanical wreck, his consciousness is shown in shambles as well, as being out of focus, tending toward hysteria rather than composure. An embittered exile denied asylum in the very world he once proudly defended, Optimus Prime enters the film as a mere afterimage of his former glory: a broken truck discovered in a broken movie theater, a wounded warrior in need of human hands, empathy, and technology to reanimate his ability to self-animate. Like Goodspeed and Lincoln Six Echo, Optimus Prime initially lacks what would qualify him as a master of flow, a self-determined agent calmly embracing the opportunity to become fully absorbed into a mission. What it takes to get him back on track, to rebuild his ability to act and speak heroically, to lead and intervene with utter concentration, is nothing less than the most fickle, messy, and contingent of all human expressions: compassion, the commitment to care and be cared for with no other reason than the recognition of need in others as much as in oneself.

Whether they display it up front or achieve it in the face of mounting challenges and discursive interludes, nothing matters more for Bay's heroes to become successful than to understand how to couple unswerving attention and resolute action. Nothing, one should add, also matters more for Bay's films to satisfy viewer expectations for narrative coherence and continuity than seeing protagonists at work who are deeply

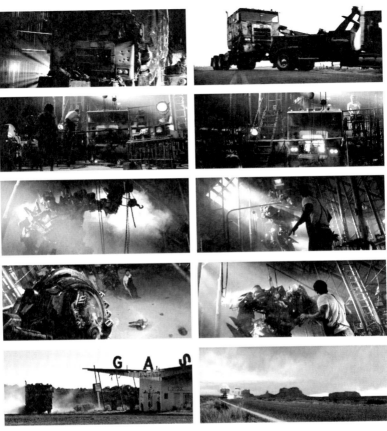

Figure 8: Finding flow III: Optimus Prime in
Transformers: Age of Extinction (2014)

absorbed in their task, their sense of flow integrating for the viewer what individual shot compositions and editing practices at first may seem to render illegible and discontinuous. The flow of Bay's heroes provides signs of continuity that his films might otherwise lack. This seems to leave us with a puzzling paradox. Most critics, with good reason, read Bay's films as spectacles designed for viewers who are no longer able to concentrate. His restless camera, his speed, his jerky editing, his elliptical narratives—all seem to envisage viewers to whom the viewing of less agitated films presents fundamental difficulties. Moreover, as some contributors to the *Urban Dictionary* have it,[31] Bay's films are

Figure 8: *Continued* |

not simply designed for viewers but are produced by a director who is deeply afflicted with attention deficit disorder: their formal organization as much as their appeal to viewers bears unmistakable marks of contemporary ADD, an inability to paying attention and controlling impulsive behavior. How, then, we must ask, is it possible to have heroes who are models of doing things for their own sake with utter concentration while appearing in films that cater to viewers for whom attention has become a fundamental problem?

A short conceptual clarification is in order to unpack this apparent paradox and present it for what it is—namely, a mere symptom of what

Malcolm McCullough discusses as a contemporary need to rethink traditional binaries of distraction and concentration and recalibrate the concept of attention for a society filled with technology, media streams, and ambient interfaces.[32] In order to understand certain generational divides between cognitive modes of approaching the world today, literary scholar Katherine Hayles has suggested distinguishing the concept of deep attention from that of hyper-attention. The former "is characterized by concentrating on a single object for long periods . . . ignoring outside stimuli while so engaged, preferring a single information stream, and having a high tolerance for long focus times."[33] Hayles's single objects can be novels, paintings, symphonies, and films that invite the reader, viewer, or listener to become fully engrossed in their flow and development at the cost of forgetting the world around her. Hyper-attention, by contrast, is "characterized by switching focus rapidly between different tasks, preferring multiple information streams, seeking a high level of stimulation, and having a low tolerance for boredom."[34] It is typical in playing video games, for instance, because games require the player to multitask, engage multiple senses at once, usually bracket the possibility of dullness, and rely on parallel streams of information. Though both modes of attention appear quite different in nature, they also share common features, not least of all the fact that both result in the subject's turning away from the everyday and in extreme situations completely ignoring basic human needs such as sleep, food, and human communication. To identify and valorize one as active and the other as passive misses the point as much as to call one intentional while identifying the other as heteronomous. Deep and hyper-attention certainly involve different structures of temporality, anticipation, and recall, of how to exist in time. Yet for both, acts of reading, viewing, or playing at their best and most intense appear autotelic. And for both attention is experienced as something that works optimally when it feels effortless.

It is impossible to imagine Bay's heroes reading a book over a prolonged period of time; in fact they might not be endowed with the gift of reading at all (as some critics may suspect). If Charles Baudelaire, according to Walter Benjamin's famous analysis, wrote poetry for readers who no longer had the patience to read poetry,[35] Bay makes films for viewers with low tolerance for both reading and viewing typical narrative cinema. It is tempting to argue that what we see at work in Bay's cinema is an effort to please hyper-attentive subjects with what to them may look like a deeply attentive mode of consciousness and action. Single-mindedly focused on one task, with great effort and yet effortlessly, the flow of Bay's heroes in action remind the video gamers of the present, in distorted and displaced form, what it once meant to concentrate deeply on one and only one thing. It might be equally tempting to turn this argument on its head. Never allowing for dull moments, Bay's flow delivers the image of hyper-attentive heroes to audiences who are willing to experience cinema as a technology of sensory immersion and absorption, a machine that recalibrates what deep attention in other arenas of cultural production once meant.

Twist this as you may, what Bay's films—his cinema of flow—actually accomplish is no less than to collapse one mode of cognitive activity and agential control into the other—that is, to unsettle the very possibility of distinguishing between hyper- and deep attentiveness. In the world we call the cinema of Michael Bay, experiences of flow on- and offscreen liquefy the very borders that cultural critics once used, and continue to use, in order to distinguish between different modalities of attending to the matters of the world. Things are being done for their own sake with great energy and yet seemingly without effort. Nothing seems to exist, both for Bay's protagonists and his spectators, outside of the task to save the (cinematic) world. Bay doesn't stop for anything: his heroes do not attend to mundane tasks such as sleeping, eating, or urinating amid the frenzy of the action, nor does the visceral agitation of Bay's sounds and images let up for a second. But is all of this news as bad as it could be?

As McCullough argues, when mapping the attentional economies of our highly mediated computational present, it is important to "note the distinction between attention as something you pay and attention as something that flows, a distinction subtler than the distinction between voluntary and involuntary."[36] Though traditionally maligned as passive, as a possible output of behavioral engineering and conditioning, flow-like modes of attention, in McCullough's perspective, play an important role today in counteracting the increasing loss of resolution, of trained skill, of tangible spatial orientation, and of embodied activity. Experiences of flow can rebuild seemingly forgotten habits, forms of inhabitation, and models of engagement with the materiality of a world that stresses the need to shape and attune our senses to our physical environment. Even if it no longer assumes the one-on-one structure associated with modes of paying attention to something, the effortlessness of flow-like attention can enable us to recognize our relationship to the ambient—the common land-, city-, image-, and soundscapes of mediated information—as a corrective to a present that is primarily dedicated to the efficiency of big data, computational abstraction, sensory overload, and neoliberal fragmentation. Effortless attention need not, but can, produce a certain ethics and politics, urging the subject to consider action and perception as something simultaneously shaping and being shaped by its environment. In so doing, it provides important resources to ask critical questions about how we want to design the physical architectures and media ecologies of the future, understood not simply as containers of action and experience but also as conditions for the possibility of conducting a good life. "Effortless attention occurs amid practiced engagement with a medium, whether the soil, a musical instrument, or your favorite design software. It becomes craft. To live well is to work well. Engaged, skillful experience makes better citizens."[37]

Agency, in Bay's films, affords attention; flow-like concentration is synonymous with action. Every single one of his heroes being or becoming an expert in their missions to warrant survival, Bay's protagonists embrace action as a craft, a skillful engagement best executed when suspending selfishness and converting oneself into a medium of autotelic purposes. Bay's heroes strategize, fight, and kill just as experienced carpenters construct tables and chairs. Few viewers might really want to share the notion of a good life coupled with this ethics of self-sustained action; even fewer might feel that the morality of Bay's heroes is more than one-dimensional and that their politics include what it would take to sustain democratic processes of deliberation and critical exchange; and no one can seriously desire to inhabit the narrative worlds exhibited on-screen, their catastrophic mayhem and violent destructiveness, and think of these worlds as models of how to live a good life. Nevertheless, whether they have it already or first need to achieve it, whether it involves unbearable pain or administers agony to others, effortless attention and flow-like action in Bay's films cultivates a certain utopian promise, a spark of transformative energy. However monstrous and distorted its momentum, Bay's flow and agitation communicates visions of a future in which human subjects can encounter ubiquitous media and technologies not as something to be feared but as reciprocal ecologies of human agency and perception, as environments to which body and thought can safely yield in a way similar to how a carpenter's chisel gently adapts to the wood's grain only to discover a whole chair inside a tree.

Time

It is often said that we live in era of too much speed. No one, many lament, takes the time to read a good book anymore, to follow the extended arc of a symphonic concert, to peruse a painting for minutes on end, or to engage complex rhetorical figures to carry out a good argument. Instead, velocity and acceleration have come to dominate all walks of life, creating pressures even expert yoga practitioners can barely breathe away. The rise of digital media is often seen as a direct conduit to this reign of tempo, this unbearable burden of being a contemporary in the twenty-first century. As they transmit more demands and distractions in ever shorter periods of time, mediated images and sounds command users to always be on and make themselves available for ongoing interruptions and interactions, communications and task-oriented interventions. In Jonathan Crary's rather bleak words: "The idea of long blocks of time spent exclusively as a spectator is outmoded. This time is far too valuable not to be leveraged with plural sources of solicitation and choices that maximize possibilities of monetization and that allow the continuous accumulation of information about the user."[38]

Michael Bay is certainly not known as a director who quarrels with the contemporary logic of 24/7 speed and acceleration. When he entered the film industry as a director of television commercials and music videos around 1990, Bay clearly knew how to aggregate considerable information and stimulation within highly compressed intervals of time. His 1993 music video for Meat Loaf, "I'd Do Anything for Love (But I Won't Do That)," commenced with a fast-paced chase sequence involving motor bikes, helicopters, and police cruisers, all staged to echo the music's beat and to energize the viewer's sense of rhythmic progress. Bay's irreverent, albeit trend-setting commercial "Got Milk?" of the same year, within the space of sixty seconds, managed to tell the story of a history buff who was unable to answer a trivia question intelligibly on time because peanut butter had incapacitated the proper functioning of his vocal organ. Caused by the gooey textures of excessive food consumption and historical fetishism, the buff's unfortunate slowness is clearly at odds with the camera's swift traversal of space, its ability to move the viewer quickly from one perspective to another and thereby motivate even the most sluggish couch potato to use time effectively and communicate promptly.

While figures of speed and acceleration inform the formal organization and visual surface of each Bay product ever since the early 1990s, no one is likely to call Bay's own career development and directorial output over the last decades sluggish either. Involving ever more complex production and postproduction operations, the first four installments of the *Transformers* franchise appeared in no more than seven years, with one additional film (*Pain & Gain*) shot before the release of the fourth *Transformers* feature. The average shot rate for more recent *Transformers* entries may have decreased a little, due to the editorial constraints imposed by 3-D formats. The films themselves, however, have turned increasingly bigger, louder, and complex in their production, design, marketing, commercial tie-in appeal, and global box office command, defining a bullish market amid abundant signs of economic deceleration after 2007. Neither Bay's films themselves nor his undertakings as director and producer will position him as a candidate for slow cinema advocates or deceleration gurus. On the contrary, Bay's world cinema is a world on steroids, a world in which everything conspires to outpace the burdens of time, history, and memory, a world that futurist speed aficionados of the early twentieth century would have loved to embrace.

In 1909 futurist poet F. T. Marinetti decreed, "We affirm that the world's magnificence has been enriched by a new beauty: the beauty of speed. A racing car whose hood is adorned with great pipes, like serpents of explosive breath—a roaring car that seems to ride on grapeshot is more beautiful than the Victory of Samothrace."[39] Michael Bay's world lives up to Marinetti's vision in its unconditional endorsement of speed, technology, and progress as much as its celebration of danger, violence, and the primordial power of courage, audacity, masculinity, and visceral interaction. Reflecting Marinetti's view, Bay's work sings to the love of ceaseless energy and fearlessness. It exalts in indefatigable movement and intoxicating speed, in continuous alertness and insomnia. It dislocates the sluggishness of museums, libraries, academies, and the contemplative life of the mind, not simply to accelerate the ticking of clocks, but to beat time at its own game, to experience—like a true futurist—omnipresent speed as the very death of time and space. Pause and sleep are foreign to Bay's heroes, the formal dynamic of his films, as much as the productivity of the director. Instead, speed figures as a first principle of individual and collective hygiene, meant to flush out whatever might prevent the individual from relishing the pleasures of movement for movement's sake.

In the eyes of many reviewers and critics, Michael Bay's need for speed typically leaves audiences hapless, either mindlessly titillated or thoroughly anaesthetized. Bay's fast-cut images, his pounding soundtracks, his hurried, albeit largely insubstantial narratives—all roll over the viewer's sensory systems and cognitive capacities like a steam engine. They provide neither space to pause and reflect nor time to place things in context and to comprehend causal connections. Instead, Bay's speed subjects the viewers' sense of time—the rhythms of their memories and anticipations, of their bodies and minds—entirely to the restless clockworks of his films, their dynamic editing as much as the ongoing motion of their protagonists, vehicles, and viewpoints. As Jim Vejvoda writes in his review of *13 Hours: The Secret Soldiers of Benghazi*: "The breathless pacing and nonstop action make [Bay's films] emotionally numbing, a merely relentless sensory onslaught."[40] To enter Michael Bay's world, then, is to permit the director to completely direct the viewer's temporal experience, to dispense the speed of mediated sights and sounds as if cinema were to serve as a powerful drug, suspending anything that could anchor this viewer in ordinary space and time. It is to follow a strangely masochistic impulse that promises redemption from the everyday by means of a mechanism that completely controls our bodies and minds with temporalities that are not our own.

Though it finds easy targets in the films of Michael Bay, the critical lament about cinema's speed as a mechanism of numb- and dumbification is certainly not new. In an effort to challenge cinematic spectatorship as an aesthetically debased form of entertainment, German film critic Wilhelm Stapel wrote as early as 1919:

Because of the rush of images, you get used to absorbing only an approxima-
tion of the impression; you do not get a clear and conscious understanding
of the image in its details. Therefore only the coarse, surprising, sensational
impressions stick. The sense for the intimate, the precise, the delicate is
lost. The patrons of cinema "think" only in garish, vague ideas. Any image
that lights up their mind's eye takes up all of their attention; they no longer
mull and reconsider it, they no longer indulge in the particularities and
the reasons.[41]

According to critics such as Stapel, film's mechanical speed was categorically at odds with human cognitive processes. It overwhelmed the senses
and undermined how the human mind sought to understand the world,
organize perception, and form evaluative judgments. Too fast, too many
impressions at once, too much rupture and discontinuity—so went the
critical refrain already a century ago to describe what many critics considered as cinema's violation of human autonomy and freedom, defined
as our ability to control and organize the flow of sensations, perceptions,
emotions, and thoughts. While the speed these early critics observed on-
screen would make most of today's viewers yawn, the twenty-first century's
critics' ire about high-speed filmmaking in general, and Bay's breathless
tempos in particular, echo nothing other than these older arguments and
normative assumptions about the nature of the very medium of film. Bay's
need for speed, as one review after the next tends to argue, prevents clear
and conscious understandings of causal action, narrative progression, and
spatial context. His rush of images mangles our desire for the intimate
and delicate. It exploits medium and viewer alike, and it thus brings to
a climax what cinema always threatened to do—namely, to sacrifice the
viewer's thoughts on the altar of unbound velocity.

   One of the central reasons why early critics of cinema abhorred the
medium for its speed simply had to do with the medium's cultural location and mode of address: early films were exhibited at fairgrounds and
projection facilities that upset nineteenth-century standards of focused
attention and absorption. Tom Gunning has famously introduced the
term "cinema of attractions" to identify the formal logic and spectatorial appeal of early motion pictures. Gunning's concept was meant to
identify how cinema in its first decade solicited conscious awareness of
the filmic image to engage the viewer's curiosity at the cost of providing integrated fictional worlds. The concept also examined how cinema

sought to stimulate astonishment by turning the viewer's attention to the machinations of cinema itself, the spectacle of putting images into motion, the special effect that was cinema long before special effects experts laid their hands on the medium.[42] According to Gunning, by 1910 the early cinema of attraction was largely succeeded by a cinema of narrative integration—that is, by films that were eager to tell self-enclosed stories and not simply to cater to the viewer's hunger for visual thrill and sensory spectacle. As Gunning himself pointed out, however, rather than die out as filmmaking gained complexity and cultural cache, the early cinema of attraction found a legitimate, albeit contained, home in the era of full-length feature filmmaking. Whenever classical and postclassical films interrupted narrative progression for the sake of showcasing spectacular sights—the dance number in a musical, the sight of a fantastic spaceship in outer space, the shootout on Main Street, the car chase in a crime film, even the close-up of a beloved star seemingly presented for our personal pleasure alone—filmmakers returned to what early cinema was all about. Gunning's cinema of attraction stresses the exhibition value of cinema, its ability to show something for the sake of showing, and his films appeal to viewers who enjoy cinema as a mechanism less to tell stories than to produce powerful illusions, magic wonders, and sensory spectacles of first rank.

It may almost sound tautological to say that Michael Bay's career is driven by the effort to return cinema to its roots in attraction, astonishment, and spectacle. Whether he shoots music videos, commercials for Victoria's Secret, or epic feature films; whether he conjures traumatic pasts or threatening futures; whether his camera shakes and rattles or creates illusions of deep 3-D space, the common denominator of his work is to engineer, with the help of twenty-first-century technologies, what animated early filmgoers as well. Bay's speed is all about play rather than meaning, spectacle rather than intimacy, exhibitionism rather than voyeurism, the viewer's "wow" rather than her "why." Or, in the words of Bruce Bennett, Leon Gurevitch, and Bruce Isaacs, "The popular image of Michael Bay is that of a puerile pyromaniac, obsessed with explosions and military-industrial technology, and it is a promotional image that he appears happy to encourage. Orson Welles once recalled that his initial impression upon visiting RKO studios in the 1940s was that they were 'the biggest electric train set a boy ever had.' It seems that Bay regards the contemporary Hollywood film set similarly, as a giant playroom, but he approaches it like a destructive child, gleefully smashing and setting fire to his toys and scribbling over the walls."[43]

In Bay's work, speed and play are two sides of one and the same coin, one needing the other, each empowering the other. Similar to the effects of methamphetamines, Bay's mayhem—understood as a technique of using violence, danger, conflict, and disaster as means to accelerate the pace of moving images—is meant to increase the viewer's heart rate, blood pressure, body temperature, and breathing rate. It is intended to induce a sense of hyperactivity and—at least metaphorically speaking—to dilate the spectator's pupils; in other words, it is meant to make us face ceaseless commotion, like a child or the viewers of early cinema, with our eyes wondrously wide open. In Bay's films the speed of play and the play of speed run up against the confines and expectations of narrative cinema. They ask the viewer to enjoy the pure passing of accelerated time even at the cost of disintegrating what made classical filmmaking viable: the trajectory of a causally determined narrative. What we come to experience when exposing our senses to Bay's speed is neither the swiftness of contemporary storytelling nor fast-track images of an individual's personal development, but first and foremost the playful thrill of showmanship, the bravura act of beating the perceived sluggishness of film history and ordinary cinematic time with each and every shot.

Contemporary sociologists argue that acceleration today results in an ever increasing and pathological desynchronization of temporal experience.[44] Compelled to make increasingly more selections and decisions in ever shorter periods of time, the twenty-first-century Western subject is no longer able to coordinate the three constitutive dimensions of temporal existence: the speed of technological innovation and communication, the velocity of larger social transformations, and the tempo of individual life trajectories and everyday calendars. Acceleration today leads to a painful disintegration of life-time and world-time, of being able to experience different temporalities as some kind of meaningful totality. What causes the true challenge to living well in the twenty-first century is not the ubiquity of speed and acceleration itself, but the fact that we no longer succeed in integrating different temporalities with one another and experience the relationships between self and world, society and subject, body and mind as resonant ones.

As little problem as Bay's films have in embracing mayhem as a site of acceleration and spectacle, as little his heroes suffer from any possible desynchronization of temporality. What defines Bay's speed as a medium of showmanship, attraction, and astonishment is that it allows protagonists and viewers alike to experience divergent tempos and temporalities as if they were part of one unified dynamic, as if the ever increasing velocity of social conditions and moving images in the digital era could serve as a mechanism to make different times and horizons of experience resonate with one another (again). Rather than fragment life-time and world-time, Bay's mayhem, or "Bayhem," showcases speed as a force that is able to reunite the incongruous temporalities of world and self, a force that is able to synchronize the very dimensions of temporality that sociologists consider as being in disarray due to the effects of too much velocity. Masters of flow, Bay's heroes embrace acceleration and danger as essential elements to experience the world as a field of resonances, one in which what exceeds subjectivity can speak to and touch on us as much as we can speak to and touch on it.

But to what extent is it actually permissible to map the resonant relations between Bay's heroes and their world of speed onto the relation between his spectators and his films? To what degree do Bay's films, as they play out high-speed spectacle and attraction against the framing power of narrative and the sluggish burdens of storytelling, really allow his viewers to be utterly in sync with what appears on-screen and—as early critics of film feared already—yield their sense of time to a world in which different dimensions of temporality all merge into one unified and reciprocal dynamic?

The answer to these questions, one might argue, depends on what you expect from seeing a Bay film in the first place. According to the majority of critics, the speed of Bayhem is designed to blow the mind out of hard-core Bay fans, wash over and away any sense of distance, and in the process make them feel as if a film's time was entirely theirs: total synchronicity at the cost of Bay's unconditional prioritization of spectacle over sense and narrative. By contrast, according to the typical Bay fan, the director's accelerated pyrotechnics emancipate cinema from the weights of interpretation, showcase contemporary cinema's ability to conjure improbable events and excessive action at its best, and in so doing invalidate the very expectations of critical critics: critics feel out of synch in the face of Bayhem, because they don't get what it is meant to do.

While it is tempting to indulge this battle for more time between speed addicts and slow critics, between aficionados of spectacle and adherents of cinematic criticality, it is even more tempting to circumvent the obvious and instead explore what both positions, contrary to their own intentions and proclamations, actually have in common. To do the latter, let me focus on a specific segment of Bay's fourth *Transformers* film, which is set in Hong Kong. It stages the final battle over the legendary Seed device, once used to energize the harvesting of life-giving metals and now in danger of falling into the hands of the Decepticons as they plan to obliterate life on Earth for the sake of their own regeneration. This culminating action sequence lasts more than thirty minutes, providing generous space and time for Bay's human protagonists to showcase their courage and resolution, for his visual effects teams to present one spectacular image after the next, for his sound engineers to envelop the audience in a highly layered and dynamically spatialized acoustical landscape, for his cinematographers to exhibit vibrant camera mobility, and for his viewers to ditch any demands for narrative development, and . . . well, let's take a look first before assessing possible effects on the viewer of this excessive festival of pyrotechnics, panicked bodies, seemingly unstoppable machinery, destructive violence, and heroic rebirth.

What Bay delivers in this particular segment, in a breathtaking succession of action, is this (fig. 9): gigantic spaceships flying over Hong Kong's cityscape, some crashing into nearby landscapes, others sucking up like colossal vacuum cleaners anything metallic from the ground, including cars, buses, trains, and cargo boats; Autobots and Decepticons chasing and shooting at each other while jumping across, and in the process demolishing, entire residential high-rises; corrupt US government agents firing their weapons at Cade Yeager and his family as the latter try to shelter the Seed from falling into the hands of Evil; Yeager and James Savoy (Titus Welliver) toppling down a building of at least fifteen stories step by step, Savoy trying to kill Yeager so as to prevent possible leaks about illegal government programs; old-style fist fights inside messy domestic interiors, concluding with an ingenious (and very American) throw of a football at the opponent's head; Transformers fighting each other on the streets amid traditional architectural settings and human multitudes attempting to escape the deadly force; architectural wreckage; vehicular wreckage; Autobots enlisting fierce metallic creatures—legendary knights called Dinobots—in their fight against the Decepticons; vehicles flying and curling through the air; humans trying to take a shot at Decepticons in spite of the inadequacy of their weaponry; Dinobots spitting fire and eating Decepticons in midair; various last-second rescues; the façades and structures of landmark towers being shredded into pieces; a city bus with a Victoria's Secret ad blown up yet not destroyed, so that its logo will remain conveniently legible; desperate car rides through a city under ongoing destruction and in the face of an entire steamship falling down from above; cunning humans trapping the Deceptions' leader in a sling of cables; the Deceptions' battleship resigned to leaving the perimeters; human protagonists and Autobots assembling at the harbor, the former celebrating a potent reaffirmation of family values, the latter proudly clarifying that their historic persecution by government policies had been foolish; and, last but not least, Optimus Prime announcing that he will hide the Seed and then starting a journey into outer space, his voice declaring royally to the film's audience: "There are mysteries to the universe we are never meant to solve. But who we are and why we are here are not among them. Those answers we carry inside. I am Optimus Prime. And this message is to my creators: leave planet Earth alone, because I am coming for you."

The sequence is loud, loaded with visual and acoustical assaults on the audience's senses, packed with spectacular visual effects and some muscular human performances, not willing to ever pause, not allowing organic or inorganic bodies to ever die. Its purpose is to assemble improbable events and incredible action like beads on a string. It moves forward at breakneck speed, although one is hard-pressed to say that action and effects intensify or progress over the course of time. And it is long. Exceptionally long. So long, in fact, that even diehard action film viewers report moments of inattention, of veering away from the action on-screen, of monotony and boredom, of desiring the end of all this because its excessive length exhausts what spectacle is meant to be all about—namely, to incite a sense of wonder for the new and unseen. The sequence is so long that film viewers at home might walk away for a while, fetch a beer from the fridge, use the restroom, or check messages on their phones and return to the viewing without feeling that

Figure 9: Wrecking Hong Kong. *Transformers: Age of Extinction* (2014)

Figure 9: *Continued*

they have missed out on anything essential. So long that Bay's speed becomes utterly slow in the process and his exhibition of spectacular novelty becomes quite old after a while.

As a point of comparison: A few years before Michael Bay turned Hong Kong into both a diegetic spectacle of destruction and a site of unprecedented Hollywood production activity in East Asia, Malaysian-Taiwanese filmmaker Tsai Ming-liang used the same city as a setting to explore a different form of slowness, of challenging the viewer's patience (fig. 10). Since the late 1990s, as if inhabiting a co-temporal, albeit utterly separate world from that of Michael Bay, Tsai has come to figure as a champion not only of East Asian art cinema as it circulates through Western art house theaters and film festivals but also of the emerging slow cinema movement, understood as a project to redefine film as a medium of contemplative stillness, a medium stressing the thickness of time, the durational, the long shot and the long take as formal methods to derail the haste of 24/7.[45] Tsai's short film *Walker* (2012) consists of twenty-one shots, spread out over little more than twenty-five minutes. In most of these takes the camera remains utterly static, inviting the viewer to attach his or her gaze to the body of a monk who does nothing but walk the streets of Hong Kong with incredible slowness, moving each foot at a rate of about thirty seconds per step. Though the duration of each individual shot is not as extended as in some of Tsai's other films—think of the glacial pace of cuts in Tsai's *Good Bye, Dragon Inn* (2003) and *Stray Dogs* (2013)—*Walker*'s slowness may at first strike the viewer as utterly anachronistic: a method to roll back the very modernity that Hong Kong embodies. The more we follow the monk's body through Hong Kong's busy streets, however, the more we come to realize that the film's uncompromising slowness provides a medium to approach an accelerated present in the mode of a contemporary. It invites the viewer to recognize and reflect on the velocity of the moment and press against the modern dominance of chronological time over the inner time of experience.

It is difficult to imagine that many have ever mentioned the names of Michael Bay and Tsai Ming-liang in one and the same sentence before. Search the internet and you will not find anything of value. It is equally hard to visualize that viewers of *Transformers: Age of Extinction* and *Walker* would ever populate the same theater lobby and exchange

Figure 10: Walking Hong Kong. Tsai Ming-liang, *Walker* (2012)

thoughts about their respective viewing experiences. And yet let's entertain the very possibility, a weird crack in two separate space-time continuums allowing Bay and Tsai viewers to communicate with each other and chat about their impressions of watching futuristic Transformers wrecking Hong Kong and timeless monks walking the streets of that city without apparent end. Once realizing that they can speak up without risking possible blunder in front of peers, isn't it possible that both sets of viewers might possibly agree that the viewing of their respective films will not really suffer from a viewer's temporary absence, inattention, or divided focus? That it appears perfectly okay to step out for a moment so as to take a leak, have a drink, answer a few emails, nap a little, or talk to a friend because their films make reentry easy? That, while "boredom" is probably not the most appropriate word to describe their state of experiencing both films' durational excesses, neither of their films' temporal order would demand utter and complete absorption in what can be seen on-screen? That both films offer attractive sights and sounds yet also give viewers ample space to consume or behold these on their own terms? That both films, no matter how fast their cuts, movements, and transitions, suspend ordinary trajectories of time and precisely in so doing allow their viewers to experience cinema as a space to sense the multiplicities of time that make up contemporary urban existence? And that, after now chatting for a few moments, it would be time again to return to their screenings and take in some more striking images, knowing all too well that no one will have missed all too much during their absence in narrative terms?

When Andy Warhol screened *Sleep* at the Cinema Theatre in Los Angeles in June 1964, around five hundred viewers were reported in attendance, eager to embark on Warhol's 321-minute feature showing nothing but the sleeping body of his friend John Giomo. Not surprisingly, it did not take long before the majority of attendees started to violate the spectatorial discipline enforced by historic conventions of traditional cinema: they talked, walked out, demanded their money back, moved restlessly around in the theater lobby. None of this, however, seemed to faze Warhol. On the contrary, he "was apparently untroubled by viewers becoming distracted, talking, or even walking in and out of the theater during the screenings of his films. And that is precisely what happened. Sympathetic audiences often lingered for a time, went into the lobby to 'hang out,' then went back into the theater after a time to continue the experience."[46] Warhol's proclaimed goal was not to discipline the viewer's temporal experience with integrated narrative forms or spellbinding spectacle. What mattered to him instead was to redefine cinema as a space inviting audiences to roam and acquaint themselves with one another, a space decompressing ordinary time while allowing attendees to engage with much more than the mere projection of a self-enclosed work.

Sleep is certainly not what Bay's thirty-five-minute sequence or Tsai's unyielding images of slow-motion walking want to induce in their viewers. Whereas the first presents Hong Kong as a site at which the future of both humanity and visual special effects is critically at stake, the latter wants to transform the erstwhile British colony into a place of contemplative looking and living, of reflecting on the speed of contemporary urban life. Although some might fall asleep after all, to do so would crucially violate the normative decorum that comes with both features discussed here, no matter how different their visual and nonnarrative economies. Still, as our counterfactual lobby discussion above might suggest, in spite of their profound differences in form, content, audience, exhibition setting, and marketing strategies, both films actually rub against the disciplinary regime that the usual cinematic conventions and screening protocols have imposed on the act of viewing. Both privilege exhibition over story, showing over telling. And in exploring the durational in very different ways indeed, both also reshuffle the temporal templates of moving-image viewership as if they actively reckon with spectators for whom sustained, single-screen, and merely consumptive acts of viewing are no longer the norm; as if both presuppose that viewers are no longer able to experience long stretches of unstructured and uninterrupted time; as if both cater to viewers who—like Warhol's highly distracted and unruly spectators—are always already accustomed to behold cinematic images at their own pace, will, and level of attention.

While Bay's films typically contract climactic action into compact windows of time and thus entertain their viewers with simulations of "real time," in particular it is the more epic sagas of the *Transformers* franchise that simultaneously open portals toward deep time that is hugely in excess of human historical records and experiences. The conflict between Autobots and Decepticons vastly preceded the counting and documenting of time on planet Earth. Transformers spaceships landed in the Arctic or on the moon long before humans had developed to lay eyes on them. In their efforts to charge their mechanical operations with organic matter, Decepticons extinguished the life of dinosaurs on Earth and thus closed an old chapter of planetary history and opened a new one. As a result, even though there is no lack of human narcissism and desire to control nature in Bay's films, his work repeatedly embeds the human within the trajectories of much larger histories: stories that are powerful enough to amend dominant traditions that place the human at the center of the making, recording, and understanding of history on planet Earth.

At a more micro level, however, such strategies of emplacing human endeavors in the deep time of planetary and geological movements never really lead to images of protagonists who are profoundly aware of their particular place in history and time. As little as Bay's heroes, in the face of spectacular dangers and challenges, take time to sleep, rest, eat, engage in leisure activities, and refuel, we also rarely witness them reading or following the news, engaging in social media activities as signs of compulsory 24/7 connectivity and "on-ness" today, or even checking their wristwatches or their phones' clock displays. Bay's heroes live deeply in time, but they have little awareness of its passing in general, its making and marking. They are, to no one's real surprise, doers rather than observers, agents rather than consumers, players rather than spectators. Though some of them adorn their domestic interiors with movie posters—think of Sam Witwicky's college dorm room featuring a poster of *Bad Boys II* (fig. 11)—it is difficult to imagine them as members of a cinematic audience, as absorbed media users, as subjects spending half their lives on cell phones and with screens instead of the physical challenges that lie ahead of them to save Earth, community, or family. Bay's heroes instead populate a world in which the realm of cinema largely expands beyond the perimeters of a movie or home theater. Witwicky uses the film poster of Bay's 2003 film not to recall a moment of astonished looking but to record unreadable messages during a period of mental instability. At best, we can envision Bay's heroes as spectators watching moving images on mobile screens and in mid-stride, understanding screens as aspects of much larger mediascapes, untroubled by missing a screenic moment or two while attending to other matters at hand. Bay's protagonists would no doubt be the first to join the lobby crowd during a screening of Warhol's *Sleep*. In fact, if confined to the cavernous space of a classical movie theater, they might have as little

Figure 11: Post-classical spectatorship.
Transformers: Revenge of the Fallen (2009)

patience with Bay's own durational display of spectacular action as they would have with watching monks walking the streets of Hong Kong.

Twenty-first-century cinephiles have come to embrace the durational takes of filmmakers such as Tsai as a medium to challenge and supersede, in the name of pensive slowness, the speed and spectacle of contemporary blockbuster filmmaking. Slow cinema advocates tend to promote glacial temporalities as art cinema's antidote to everything Bay represents. And yet there might be good reasons to understand both—the slow and unmoving image of the walker and the fast-cut action sequence running for more than thirty minutes—as opposite sides of the same coin. Both emerged within the same historical context. Both respond to similar cultural conditions. Both engage with the overburdening power of contemporary speed and seek to rework it by means of deflating the narrative drive of typical storytelling. Both displace the teleological arc of narrative progress for the sight of wondrous, awe-inspiring events, recalling the exhibitionary force of early cinema as much as the undisciplining of viewership associated with 1960s practices of expanded cinema such as Warhol's. First and foremost, however, both provide potent answers to the questions raised by the rise of a new type of spectator since the mid-1990s, a spectator most rigorously conceptualized in Laura Mulvey's reflections on how digital technologies have come to empower spectators to control the flow of cinematic time on their own terms, freeze individual images, or repeat entire sequences so as to dissolve the forward power of narrative, fiction, and cinema's illusion of movement.[47]

According to Mulvey, one of the most important developments in recent moving-image culture is the advent of what she calls the "possessive spectator": a viewer empowered by digital technology to delay or freeze narrative temporality in order to consume individual images most intensely. Possessive viewership suspends the presumed narrative laws of cause and effect. It willfully interrupts a film's narrative drive in the hope of gaining control over the appearance of desired objects and thus turning acts of viewing into means of fetishistic pleasure. "The possessive spectator commits an act of violence against the cohesion of a story, the aesthetic integrity that holds it together, and the vision of its creator."[48] While such violence may express desire for mastery and sadistic power, at its best it may actually also remind the viewer of cinema's uncanny power to show the past as present and to reanimate the dead. In its effort to delay narrative flow, possessive spectatorship thus has the potential to make us experience cinema's indexical mummification of change, its mysterious embalming of time. "In the act of halting the flow of film, then returning it to its movement and vitality, the possessive spectator inherits the long-standing fascination with the human body's mutation from animate to inanimate and vice versa."[49]

Bay's *Transformers: Age of Extinction*, like Tsai's *Walker*, is designed with viewers in mind for whom possessive spectatorship—the willful manipulation of cinematic temporality for the sake of isolating individual attraction—has become the norm. Rather than simply lament the state of contemporary viewership as cinema's fall from grace, both films set out to work with, and rework, present modes of viewing, well aware that Warhol's restless spectators of the 1960s have become the stock of twenty-first-century moving-image culture. Ackbar Abbas once described Hong Kong, in its unique postcolonial position of relative economic prosperity and political dependence, as a culture of melancholic minds and accelerated economies: "If you cannot choose your political leaders, you can at least choose your own clothes. We find therefore not an atmosphere of doom and gloom, but the more paradoxical phenomenon of *doom and boom*: the more frustrated or blocked the aspirations to 'democracy' are, the more the market booms."[50] Representing seemingly opposite poles of global cinema today, both Bay and Tsai embrace Hong Kong not simply as a setting to suspend cinema's drive of narrative time and to invite the viewer to acts of possessive looking, but as a background to feature urban doom and destruction as a stimulus for new and different ways of looking at cinematic images, as a boom expanding cinema beyond its twentieth-century horizons. What fascinates both Bay's and Tsai's viewers alike are sights of bodies hovering somewhere between the animate and inanimate; images that play with the passing of time without surrendering physical transformations to the exigencies of narrative temporality; scenes whose choreographies appeal to fetishistic impulses and desires for exhibitionary attraction; motion pictures that afford the viewer some control over the progress of time and possibly define boredom as a site of productivity. For both directors, cinema today is less about telling stories than it is about featuring motion itself. And for both, movement on-screen appears truly wondrous because it is seen against the backdrop of a possible standstill, of death and destruction. If cinema no longer holds the power to make you sit still for hours on end and stare at one screen alone, at least offer the viewer something he or she can choose to possess temporarily before turning to other business. If traditional narrative arcs no longer hold our undivided attention, turn doom into boom and, like Warhol, allow viewers to take in images at their own pace, to experience cinema as an event rather than a display of self-enclosed works, and to move through alternating phases of de- and re-synchronizing with the movements on-screen without feeling the need to know and be with all projected images at all times.

To be sure, not one of Michael Bay's films is thinkable without the figure of the hero running up against some clock and deadline to rescue him and others. Time is always on the run, so much so that no one ever has time to check the time, and daily routines and rituals appear all but suspended. However, whereas Bay's protagonists appear in perfect synchronicity with the temporalities of the world, the expansive action sequences of his films increasingly ask and allow viewers to drift in and out of these films' temporal arcs, to relax from the demands of both classical narrative cinema and the blockbuster spectacle film and instead consider cinema, with all of its different sites and platforms today, as a space of ambient stimulation and attention, as a site to be approached, inhabited, and possessed in a way that is similar to how we approach, appropriate, inhabit, and navigate an architectural structure. In spite of all of its hurry and urgency, then, time in Bay's films has the tendency to become and be space. It moves. And it doesn't. It speeds forward. And it reiterates the always same. It flies like an arrow. And it circles like the eddy in a river. It washes over our heads as much as it allows us to pause, look elsewhere, withstand its drive. Bay's films thus ask us to redefine how we have come to theorize a spectacle's impact on the viewer. They not only emblematize conditions under which cinema can be found everywhere in society and society has become cinema with other means. As importantly, they also undock our understanding of viewership from the idea of monadic spectators silently trying to master each and every work in its entirety. They redefine cinema, like it or not, as a cultural technology that no longer serves the purpose of pleasing or educating the crowd, but of articulating this crowd in space and time; and they replace—as Hito Steyerl has argued with regard to the exhibition of moving-image work such as Tsai's in art museums and at international art fairs—the sovereign gaze of the typical spectator with incomplete, fractured, mobile, at times common, and at times individualized practices of viewing.[51] Bay's cinema of speed is post-representational. Like Tsai's, it caters to viewers who find cinema everywhere and whose gaze is neither solely individual nor fully collective. In its temporal incompleteness and contingency, it is common and can be edited into principally unpredictable sequences and combination. Although many more than 100 million people worldwide may say that they have seen *Transformers: Age of Extinction*, no one can claim to have seen the same film.

No matter how post-representational his cinema may be, no sight allegorizes Bay's philosophy of speed and time more graphically than the one of worm-like Decepticons drilling their way through natural or man-made landscapes. They often literally appear out of nowhere. Their force is unstoppable due to their rotational drive; their sheer appearance—similar to what scares many about sightless critters—incites terror already, because, for them, perceiving the world is to approach it exclusively through the act of (destructive) touch. They are constantly on the move, never pause, yet have no clear sense of direction, no goal other than flattening whatever lies in their path. Unlike most other Transformers, good or evil, Bay's drilling bots are void of intention and any trace of (artificial) intelligence. They are pure drive and unremitting speed. They rotate for the sake of rotation. They destroy for the sole sake of destruction, with no other aim or idea attached to it. If they were human, they would represent—nay, *be*—the perfect embodiment of Freud's id, unfettered from anything that channels drives and desires into forms of sociability. If they, unlike most other Transformers, had anything anthropomorphic about them, we would have to think of them as ambassadors of the unconscious, turned loose and entering the world of objects as if our minds had completely abandoned any hope to be masters in our own houses.

A most monstrous return of society's repressed, the Decepticon Driller (fig. 12), during the epic battle over Chicago in *Transformers: Dark of the Moon* (2011), is everything futurism always wanted but even in its most aggressive visions did not allow itself to be. Driller's speed is irresistible and unrelenting. It knows of neither fear nor moral obligations. It drills itself through office towers and urban infrastructures, always on the attack, always eager to flatten any sign of civilizing prowess and cultural accomplishment. It exalts in aggressive action, feverish insomnia, the punch and the slap for the only reason of clearing the ground for an unknown future. Void of visual perception, it touches upon things to destroy and destroys to touch. It has no sense for any difference between interior and exterior spaces, penetrates entire architectural structures without pause and hesitation, and manages to make high-rises tilt or collapse as if they were made of paper. Pure speed, drive, and power, Driller is the nemesis of anything static and settled, the monuments of modernity as much as the emasculating sites of civilized behavior. Marinetti's cheer of 1909 would be written on Driller's banner were it able to read and write: "And so, let the glad arsonists with charred fingers come! Here they are! Here they are! . . . Go ahead! Set fire to the shelves of the libraries! . . . Turn aside the course of the canals to flood the museums! . . . Oh, the joy of seeing all the glorious old canvases floating adrift on the waters, shredded and discolored! . . . Seize your pickaxes, axes, and hammers, and tear down, pitilessly tear down the venerable cities!"[52]

Lisa Purse has read the figure of Driller as one example of what she calls the "rotational aesthetics" of Michael Bay's cinema: a cinema not only coupling movement to power but also, like Marinetti's poetry, exalting in fantasies of infinite kineticism and phallocentric mastery:

> The recurrence across the franchise of villainous, tentacled robots whose very shape and motion displays their primary function to destructively penetrate any object, along with the gendered specificity of Driller's mechanical take on

Figure 12: Driller at work. *Transformers: Dark of the Moon* (2011)

the *vagina dentata* myth, exemplify the extent to which these non-humanoid Decepticons' perceived threat is dramatised by figures of rotation rooted in hyperbolic, normatively gendered visions of castration and penetration. The deployment of the trope of rotation in these action sequences visually configures power persistently in terms of an outwardly displayed capacity and desire to penetrate; this is mastery as a (frequently slow motion) "screwing" of the space of action, or of opponents' bodies.[53]

Borrowing a phrase from Michael Bay himself, Purse goes on to describe Driller, as so many other rotational figures in Bay, as a sign not only of violent fantasy but also of a general aesthetics of "fucking the frame," of unhinging and drilling through the borders of the cinematic image so as to affect the viewer at a visceral level.

As much as rotational figures in Bay are designed to fuck the frame, however, they also reveal the ambivalent nature of Bay's entire credo of speed, energy, and futuristic progressivism. I have written elsewhere about how in Marinetti's works the praise of speed, precisely because it wants to explode traditional templates of time and space, ends up sacrificing the contingent and unpredictable on the altar of what is unremitting and relentless about velocity and progress itself.[54] Instead of unlocking the future as a realm of unscripted possibilities, speed and ceaseless motion destroy what allows us to map progress and speed in the first place and result in conditions under which mechanical powers trump the vagaries of human existence, and manic repetition absorbs any desire for difference. All about speed and progress, Marinetti endorses an eternal return of the new and a perpetual renewal of the old; he folds circular and linear time into one mythic vision of total synchronicity, one in which planetary, technological, and human time all become one.

Bay's rotational aesthetics is heir to this collapsing of different registers of time. It fuses the circular and the linear, progress and repetition, the trajectorial and the erratic, power and awe into one single stream. Driller fascinates because he all at once spins and moves, turns forward and in circles, operates at high speed and grinds everything to a halt. Like Marinetti's aesthetics of speed, Driller's rotational aesthetic echoes strategies and micro-tactical maneuvers of contemporary warfare, in this case the "walking through walls"—the horizontal transgression, destruction, reorganization, and subversion of human habitats—that architect Eyal Weizman sees at the heart of today's urban military encounters.[55]

As it seeks to fuck the frame with each and every shot, Bay's rotational aesthetics demands that the viewer choose speed as a means to forfeit our very ability to choose, to expose ourselves to spectacles of velocity as a means to escape the painful desynchronization of time we associate with too much speed to begin with. As we have seen in the preceding pages, however, Bay's viewers might be more resilient to this than most critics, and Bay himself, presume. Rather than being screwed (up) by the restless action on-screen, they may increasingly find meaning and pleasure, not in images outspeeding contemporary speed at all costs, but in windows of narrative delay and suspension in which boredom, as in Warhol or Tsai, may reemerge as a welcome space, as a precondition, of curiosity and the unpredictable, of impromptu encounters and wondrous experiences.

Matter

The opening shot of Bay's *Pain & Gain* shows bodybuilder Daniel Lugo (Mark Wahlberg) performing a rather unusual exercise routine (fig. 13). His feet are hooked into a metal contraption attached to a huge advertising sign. Each aerial sit-up allows him not only to work out his abs but also to look straight into the face of a weight lifter, the latter's graphic image reminiscent of design strategies known from New Deal America in the 1930s as well as the totalitarian aesthetic of Soviet Russia, Nazi Germany, and Fascist Italy. Long before the film's narrative leads us further into the contorted mind-set of Lugo, for whom the sculpting of the male body perfectly embodies the American dream of individual self-improvement, the opening shot thus already confronts the viewer with a curious scene of corporeal rigidity, discipline, and self-idealization. "My name is Daniel Lugo and I believe in fitness," we hear him say in a voice-over, justifying the uncompromising nature of his work ethic as much as the vision that nature needs to be shaped into quasi-geometric structures in order to gain meaning and value. Mirroring himself in a futuristic image drawn from the past, Lugo views bodybuilding as communicating the will's triumph over what is amorphous about the ordinary body. A Nietzschean strategy of radical self-assertion, his workout routine casts into reliable form what appears unbearably contingent, messy, and unpredictable about pure matter.

A few minutes into *Transformers: Age of Extinction*, the viewer is exposed to a giant billboard amid the Texan countryside, a shot also used effectively in the film's initial trailer and marketing campaign (fig. 13). "Remember Chicago" we read in capital letters that are set against the backdrop of the city's well-known skyline, the faint image of an American flag taking up half of the display space. The sign recalls, for diegetic and nondiegetic viewers alike, the previous installment of the *Transformers* franchise, in whose final hour the battle between Autobots and Decepticons transformed the Windy City into a landscape of shapeless ruins, a site of utter destruction that future generations could only refer to as image and immaterial memory. Here, however, the image of Chicago is coupled with an additional order: "Report Alien Activity" we read in the lower left corner, while a phone number on the right is meant to direct such reporting and help prevent another attack on the material infrastructures

Figure 13: Bodies that matter. From top:
Pain & Gain (2013); *Transformers: Age of
Extinction* (2014)

of American life. In 2014 that phone number led curious viewers to a pre-recorded voice message warning about the danger of Transformers. It also urged any caller to visit a webpage that basically served as an advertising mechanism for the entire franchise. Once a clever fusion of diegetic and nondiegetic worlds, of filmic and non-filmic matter, the phone number was eventually taken over by a phone sex hub directing needy customers to various possible objects of pleasure. Hooked to the Sun Gym's advertising sign, Lugo would have surely liked this: the body's return, the return of the real, into the space of the symbolic, a space fictionalizing the real in the wake of a fictional demolition of a city's body. Yet being on death row since 1998, the real Lugo himself has probably little opportunity to call the number on display in search of physical gratification. And his embodiment on-screen, Mark Wahlberg, has beefed-down his sculpted body after the making of *Pain & Gain* and moved on to different projects, including the making of *Transformers: Age of Extinction* and *Transformers: The Last Knight*, released in June 2017.

Ours is an age of often lamented dematerialization. The dusk of the Anthropocene depletes natural resources at unprecedented speeds and scales. We are told, however, that life increasingly moves into nonmaterial spaces, that most of it is lived in electronic circuits, screen-based environments, and virtual habitats. While their bodies struggle with increasing obesity, kids progressively lose touch with touch, with their ability to navigate material landscapes, handle objects with care, assess their own motility, and sense the physical world as something that may resonate with their own bodies. Digital media not only killed video and radio; they also obliterated nature, sensory perception, and the physical as grounds of human practice and interaction. Bay's billboard shots at once invoke this lament, but after some more careful analysis also unsettle it. At first sight, they articulate resolute claims for the obstinacy of the material world, even in or after its very disappearance. In both shots, physical entities—the sculpted muscle, the urban landscape—are said and shown to matter. Moreover, both shots wrap this saying and showing in nostalgic sentiments, marking what we see as something that belongs to a pre-digital past. An old television antenna fills the foreground of the opening shot of *Pain & Gain*; a massive cargo train rolls up on the right toward the camera in the "Remember Chicago" shot of *Transformers: Age of Extinction*: both technologies of communication and transport whose function young viewers in the second decade of the twenty-first century may no longer really remember, both referring the audience to industrial times in which digital media had not yet taken over and analog technologies still served humans to make the world their own. The prominent use of billboards in both shots of course complicates this nostalgia, or, better, it exposes the nostalgia as nostalgia, as spectacle, as object of consumption. Whether the sign sells robust bodies as a project or remembers the destruction of material infrastructures as lack and traumatic wound, in both shots the medium of the display board is essential to uphold the claims of the physical and sensory world. In both, media are shown as matter as much as matter is unthinkable without and is revealed by its medium. Both shots display mediation as no less than an ontological fact. Media define and shape how humans recall the past, envision the future, and, in so doing, seek to inhabit the present as embodied subjects. Media are elemental to what it means to be human in Michael Bay's world cinema.

Blockbuster action cinema, as we have come to know it since the late 1970s, but even more so since the rise of spectacular digital effects in the 1990s, is often thought to be entirely about the strength, muscular resolution, physical prowess, pain, and corporeal sacrifice of the male body. The central goal of action cinema is to display men's bodies prevailing over other bodies, over matter, because they understand how to embrace technologies, weapons, and vehicles as servile media of teleological action. Media, according to this understanding, extend the male body into the world, harden it, provide armor. To succeed in the world is to rule over minds and matter as much as to understand media as essential keys to do so, as tools whose nature is never more than being instrumental. Action films are celebrations, less of what Nietzsche called the "will to power" than of what Theodor W. Adorno and Max Horkheimer when commenting on Odysseus's cunning considered the quasi-anthropological pathology of Western civilization—namely, its privileging of strategic reason and goal-oriented action, its transformation of both inner and outer nature into a source, a medium, of self-maintenance and domination.[56] Like Homer's survival artist Odysseus, action heroes as we know them succeed whenever they understand how to transform anything and everything into a tool of their needs, desires, and missions—into objects of self-preservation. In the world of the action hero, even mimesis and playfulness, the beautiful image of a landscape or the seductive sound of a song, have no other function but to serve the cause of the (male) body's will to dominate matter, the latter understood as inherently passive and void of self-determination.

None of this is surprising, even if few viewers might really be willing to contemplate the metaphysics of action while marveling at how a Schwarzenegger, Willis, Stallone, Statham, Dwayne Johnson, Cruise, or Diesel plow their way through one challenge after another. None of it really requires any retelling were it not for the fact that Michael Bay's cinematic world, more unknowingly than with deliberation, offers repeated glimpses of a categorically different understanding of matter, medium, and mind; of how humans may approach and be approached by the materiality of the world; and of how they may define life at its best, not in opposition to what is unfree about matter and media but by recognizing that objects and media, bodies and architectures, technologies and nature have agency themselves. Earlier in this book, I compared what we call "A Michael Bay Film" to what zoologists, media theorists, and cultural critics call swarms and assemblages: dynamic constellations in which intentions are always in competition and coalition with other strivings; groupings of diverse elements that move jointly as if there were no center of control and power. Now I want to extend such a post-humanist rethinking of authorship in the age of cinematic world-building to the role of objects, of matter and media, the matter of media and the mediation of matter, in Bay's films themselves. Though action and disaster film genres as we know them appear unthinkable without their plots being anchored in strong human intentions—the will to survive, to prevail, to triumph, to impress—Bay's cinema repeatedly toys with the idea of a post-anthropomorphic ecology of things, of vibrant matter endowed with agential powers. In its very eagerness to display the nature of matter as something that, far from eschewing mediation, requires media to reveal itself, Bay's films—unwittingly—depict the late Anthropocene era as a world in dire need of sensibilities that find "a world filled not with ontologically distinct categories of beings (subjects and objects) but with variously composed materialities that form confederations."[57] Three types of materiality repeatedly stand out in Bay's world: architectural volumes, the human body, and planetary objects. All of them feature matter as a medium in its own right. All of them emancipate agency from the exclusive resort of the human mind.

And all of them urge us to move beyond worn concepts of nature as the other of technology, culture, and civilization. Although it would be foolish to claim Bay and the carbon-heavy footprints of his productions are intended for contemporary agendas of sustainability, his films beg us to probe the extent to which they unsettle historical paradigms that pivot on how humans have come to use technology to fundamentally change the Earth and articulate their sovereignty over things and objects considered dumb, lifeless, and without any sense of agency whatsoever. Let's go probing, then.

Bay's Architectures

Architectural structures help define human distances in space; they choreograph habits, arrange relations, and direct movements. As it configures space in time, architecture operates as a scaffolding for what we know, how we act, and what we sense. It provides high-resolution infrastructures for today's low-resolution experience of flickering images, ceaseless information flows, and electronically mediated interactions.[58] And yet to think of architectural structures as something that simply exist and run in the background does not imply that we should not consider them as media of sorts. On the contrary, modernist architects often designed buildings as stationary framing devices allowing sedentary or mobile users to perceive the surrounding world as a series of quasi-cinematic perspectives and sequences; they built the perceptual condition of twentieth-century mass media such as film straight into material configurations.[59] Moreover, anyone recalling the fact that well into the nineteenth century elemental forces such as air, water, fire, and earth themselves were considered media will not find it unwarranted to think of built space as a medium as well. "Media," writes John Durham Peters, "are vessels and environments, containers of possibility that anchor our existence and make what we are doing possible."[60] A downtown high-rise certainly matches this definition as much as a suburban duplex, a prehistoric cave dwelling, or a tent used during a weekend camping trip.

Bay's world certainly abounds with architectural structures whose materiality—hidden or plainly visible—shapes the protagonists' being in the world. To be sure, often much of what we see as built space in his films exists solely for the purpose of being destroyed. It needs to be flattened, sacrificed, or overcome to reboot the operations of life. Bay's architecture is "warchitecture": habitats built for destruction and displacement, buildings meant to be unbuilt.[61] Suburban domestic spaces, in this respect, fare as badly as corporate towers or postindustrial infrastructures. The Witwickys' Californian domicile in the first installment of the *Transformers* franchise gets as much smashed amid epic battles over the future of humanity as Cade Yeager's farmhouse and engineering lab in Texas does in *Transformers: Age of Extinction*. Little is left of Chicago and Shanghai after Autobot warriors refute the genocidal schemes of Decepticon invaders. Japanese planes turn ships, barracks, airports, hospitals, and residential areas of Hawaii into debris in *Pearl Harbor*. In the *Bad Boys* franchise, a fierce shootout transforms the entrance area of Mike Lowrey's upper-class apartment complex in Miami into a ruin, while Marcus Burnett's middle-class family home suffers various (self-inflicted) flooding problems. Several major metropolitan hubs across the globe, including Manhattan, suffer complete destruction when meteors take aim at planet Earth in *Armageddon*. And even Alcatraz, symbol of impenetrable stability in time and space, is shown as a place that is much less secure and self-sustaining than ever thought before; though its walls remain intact during *The Rock*, its perimeters are not immune to various breaches, and its foundations are much more porous than state authorities had initially envisioned.

It is clear that in Bay's films built space is never safe, never considered a bulwark against the entropy of time. Few of Bay's protagonists, at the end of their respective adventures, are able to return to where they started. Unlike Odysseus's Ithaca, their homes have been devastated in the process of the narrative; no one is really awaiting their homecoming to what once was a primary site of intimacy, orientation, and being in the world. Architecture, writes Peter Zumthor, "has a special relationship with life. I do not think of it primarily as either a message or a symbol, but as an envelope and background for life which goes on in and around it, a sensitive container for the rhythms of footsteps on the floor, for the concentration of work, for the silence of sleep."[62] Bay's heroes rarely move as if they needed backgrounds to enable their lives, their steps, their work. Because neither sleep nor leisure appear necessary or in reach for them, we rarely see them crave sensitive containers facilitating what they may consider life in the first place. Life, as they know it, is best conducted in the open, anticipating that the materials and crafts that provide sustainable structures, resonances, and envelopes for human bodies may never be as lasting as designed.

For the majority of Bay's heroes, architecture serves neither as message and symbol, nor, as it may appear, as a method to compose space with physical materials and thereby create zones of relative stability and meaningful inhabitation. If we asked them, they would have not much to say about what kind of structures and infrastructures should replace the sites of destruction. For them, architecture is what needs to be obliterated to create space for human action and heroism. At heart, they love empty space as a precondition to move forward, to move at all, and to prove the value of their resolute interventions. With some exceptions confirming the norm, Bay's heroes represent what Walter Benjamin with a certain fascination called the "destructive character": "The destructive character sees nothing permanent. But for this very reason he sees ways everywhere. Where others encounter walls or mountains, there, too, he sees a way. But because he sees a way everywhere, he has to clear things from it everywhere. Not always by brute force; sometimes by the most refined. Because he sees ways everywhere, he always stands at a crossroads. No moment can know what the next will bring. What exists he reduces to rubble—not for the sake of rubble, but for that of the way leading through it."[63]

Designed as a playground for destructive characters in Benjamin's sense, Bay's world cinema, one might conclude, has little to offer viewers who are eager to hear and see architectural objects speak to and look back at their users' presence. If Bay's protagonists secretly or not so secretly love rubble so as to fancy ways into the open, then there is little hope to encounter architectural structures that resonate with those who inhabit them. After all, destructive characters have no real need and patience for buildings that allow their users to touch upon them as much as be touched by them, nor for material configurations that enable dwellers to be in tune with their surroundings in a way that is similar to how tuning forks pick up the vibration of other sounding bodies and begin to swing on their own. The organ harvesting factory in *The Island* stands out in this respect (fig. 14). It's a cold, abstract, clean, and unwelcoming space, situated underground somewhere in the desert in the American Southwest. Although not aware of their status as mere clones awaiting future organ extraction, the site's inhabitants are monitored at all times.

Figure 14: Architecture as a medium. *The Island* (2005)

Integrating work and leisure as if no difference existed, the building functions like a giant panopticon. Its electronic surveillance instruments constantly check on physical as much as psychological, exterior as much as interior signs of possible dysfunction. Fully aware that they are being watched and traced even during sleep, the structure's dwellers have come to accept the absence of any boundary between the public and the private as a quasi-natural order of the day.

To the outside eye, however, they move, eat, work, and communicate like Pavlovian dogs, ubiquitous observation ensuring that they act as if being handled by remote controls. To keep everyone in line, the building entertains them with giant monitors and on-screen lottery shows. Electronic media promise exotic pleasures on the film's titular island even though, as the viewer is later to find out, the selection process is by no means random, and to be selected simply means to be picked out for organ extraction—in other words, death. Moreover, holographic machines produce powerful illusions of what may lie beyond the building's windows and perimeters, obscuring the structure's subterranean location with pleasant natural imagery. All in all, *The Island*'s organ plant offers a perfect virtual reality machine. It not only provides what can be seen and sensed with nearly seamless perfection, but it also engineers how its dwellers see and sense their surroundings, how they perceive their own perception and synchronize it with what they know about the past and envision for the future.

Blown up in the very end of the film to liberate its slave population, *The Island*'s cloning facility embodies what could be seen as a sign of modernist architecture gone fundamentally sour. As it levels any meaningful difference between advanced media technologies, screen-based images, physical walls, and windows, the building recalls early twentieth-century fantasy of architecture as a medium that is able to frame animated views onto the world, similar to how early cinema projected moving images. As important, the building pretends to offer a container that fully anchors its inhabitants' existence and enabling whatever they believe to be seeing, sensing, and doing, thus aspiring to a concept of architecture as a quasi-elemental medium, as a technique for engineering and reengineering our entire habitat. Nevertheless, the sole purpose of *The Island*'s bold architectural foray is of course to dupe its inhabitants, to make slaves feel as if they were contended dwellers, as if dwelling under the conditions of advanced technological interventions were still possible. What Bay's clones, in the absence of knowing any better, consider a resonant ecology of life, a medium no different from the functions ancient thinkers ascribed to air, earth, and water, is nothing other than a deceptive spectacle, a special effect that massages minds and emotions for the sake of producing airtight submission. Once meant to dominate the mere matter of nature in order to showcase the superiority of human rationality and power, technology in *The Island* now also entertains the nonhuman with glimpses of humanity in order to advance its course. Resonance—the feeling of being in sync with the matter of one's environment—becomes deeply repressive. The building's media, the building's status as a medium, are as total as they are totalitarian.

But wait.

What initially triggers Lincoln Six Echo's rebellion against the system results from nothing other than a glitch within the plant's dual transformation of architecture into a medium of totalitarian control and of body matter into a commodity of first rank. Though he is a product of advanced genetic engineering, Lincoln Six Echo has dreams he shouldn't have, shows physical responses and traits of emotions that are not part of his program, begins to perform conformity and thereby attests to its limitations, and engages with fellow clones as if *Blade Runner*'s Roy Batty had reemerged from the dead and spread his message that androids might be more human than humans. Lincoln Six Echo's revolt is a revolt of matter, of nature, against the modern hubris of instrumental reason. It articulates no less than a monstrous return of the repressed, playing out what the plant's leaders, managers, scientists, and sponsors believe to have in full control but cannot fail to do so. Glitches reveal the medium as medium. They expose the extent to which media, as much as they are part of the world of human action and consciousness, are also part of the world of nature, are matter themselves. Much more than a mere sign of a malfunction, glitches lay bare the properties and specificities of their medium, display them as the material condition—the quasi-natural, albeit historically constituted substrate—of the possibility of meaning-making and experience.[64]

His desire for human sensibilities the outcome of a glitch, Lincoln Six Echo—like all the other freed slave workers and organ producers at the very end of the film—has no cause to believe he could ever surpass his existence as a genetically engineered being. What he and they can hope for, however, is a future in which conventional boundaries between the human and the nonhuman, body and machine, nature and technology are no longer seen as radically distinct as humans themselves tend to presume to uphold their sovereignty over matter. While the plant's modernist mingling of matter and media is destroyed, the slaves' final movement into the openness of the desert at first seems to articulate the utter and quite conventional triumph of nature over artifice, the elemental over the mediated, biology over technology. In truth, however, unknowing to them as much as perhaps its director, what we come to witness is no less than a powerful confirmation that nature cannot do without mediation and that matter itself needs technological media to come into the open. Bay's clones will remain clones forever. What truly matters, for them as much as for us, is to create environments—infrastructures and ecologies of life—in which we can freely realize that we cannot do without media and to use this insight as a basis to develop a more hospitable version of nature than the version that instrumental reason has turned into a mere object of control and domination. The idea of nature as unmediated matter is long dead and done with. Build a better one.

It is no surprise, then, that some innovative international architects have allowed Michael Bay's aesthetic to inform their design and practice. The Bolivian architect Freddy Mamani Silvestre, who is quite hostile to drawing formal blueprints or working out of stationary offices, has developed numerous futuristic penthouses and commercial structures near La Paz that combine motifs from Aymara weaving and Andean temples with the look of Bay's *Transformers* films, as if to emphasize the instability and malleability of architectural structures, their ongoing recasting of the past for an unpredictable future.[65] Michael Jantzen's so-called M House, a 90-square-meter one-bedroom cottage, combines a structural steel frame and panels made of composite concrete so as to provide a habitat in the California desert that can easily be assembled and reassembled according to location, need, and purpose. Its robotic shape displays its function—endless variability—on its formal sleeve: "This Transformer House has adjustable legs attached to load bearing footpads that are capable of being sited anywhere without the need for site preparation. . . . A team of four people can easily assemble M House in just one week. The force of simplicity in architecture always leads to surprising outcomes, don't you agree?"[66] And, finally, in the "Bird Island" project in Kuala Lumpur, flexible exterior skins made out of silicone-covered glass fabric create at once airy, peaceful, and adjustable environments for their residents that can easily be adapted to their surrounding waterfront landscapes, the growths of trees, the shifting of water levels. Its insider name explicitly absorbs Bay's industrial futurism into the rhetoric of sustainability after all: "Eco Transformer Architecture."[67]

Bay's Bodies

Bodybuilding, it has often been said, develops muscular structures in order to compensate for an underdeveloped ego. It fortifies and extends the boundaries of the body, at once hardens the flesh and pushes it beyond its initial margins, so as to recenter a fragile self within the cocoon of hypermasculinity. But as Alan Klein has forcefully argued, his eyes on the use of mirrors in contemporary gym and workout culture, "Narcissus fell completely in love with his reflection. The bodybuilder would like to, but can't. Inside that body is a mind that harbors a past in which there is some scrawny adolescent or stuttering child that forever says, 'I knew you when . . . .' The metamorphosis is doomed to remain incomplete."[68] Scrawny youngsters, disguised as masculine champs, widely populate the world of Michael Bay's cinema, both in front of and behind the camera, on and vis-à-vis the screen. No matter how eagerly his heroes sacrifice themselves for larger causes, infrequent are those who are entirely free of narcissistic motivations, rare those who are not haunted by backgrounds that may possibly question their masculine stances. No single film, however, is more explicit than *Pain & Gain* about the psychological and ideological makeup of contemporary body work, its three muscular protagonists acting as if hardened biceps and rippling six-packs indicated the highest stage of individual, moral, and social development. And no single film, at the same time, leaves us with a more puzzling picture of how in Bay's cinema populist appeal and narrative intention often end up at loggerheads with each other, the former displacing whatever the latter might initially seek to communicate.

Set in the mid-1990s, *Pain & Gain* tells the story of Daniel Lugo, a recently released convict, who works as a personal trainer at the Sun Gym in Miami (fig. 15). Tired of his existence at the bottom of the

Figure 15: The politics of fitness. *Pain & Gain* (2013)

social ladder, Lugo recruits two fellow bodybuilders, Adrian Door-bal (Anthony Mackie) and Paul Doyle (Dwayne Johnson), to kidnap one of his clients, Victor Kershaw (Tony Shalhoub), with the intention of redistributing his wealth. Not really to anyone's surprise, however, throughout the film the kidnappers' limited intelligence creates obstacles to make their plan succeed, with Bay trying to portray their haplessness in what is meant to be a comical mood. Scenes of torture alternate with macabre sequences in morgues, verbal and visual puns about sex toys give way to accidental death due to the uses of horse tranquilizers, moments of fateful misidentification exchange for not so humorous acts of fake identity. Lugo and his comrades represent what, three years after the film's release, drove millions of voters into the arms of populist presidential candidates whose neoliberal agendas directly linked wealth to personal achievement and considered economic hardship a mere symptom of a loser's attitude. For Lugo and his buddies, to work out and buff the body is to pursue the American dream of self-management and self-perfection, of rugged individualism as the primary source of freedom and success. Benjamin Franklin and Max Weber would be proud of them, minus their criminal activity. For Lugo and company, time indeed is money, their work ethic no less uncompromising, structured by ascetic impulses, and in search for redemption than the one that situated Protestants as the spirited godfathers of modern capitalism. According to Lugo, the effort to transform bodies into muscular armors pursues Weber's regime of inner-worldly asceticism in a new key. The addiction and obsession that comes with it—"My name is Daniel Lugo and I believe in fitness"—recast body work as an analogue of neoliberal entrepreneurialism, its language of deregulation as much as its destruction of existing fabrics of sociability.

In their discussion of Bay's dynamic cinematography and play with the technological sublime, both Mark Bould and Lisa Purse point out that the high-speed conversion of Transformers from one vehicular body into another typically escapes legibility. Discussing a particularly striking example in the first *Transformers* film, Purse writes: "Across the sequence, the changes in Optimus's structure accelerate so that they become difficult to discern, as chunks of metal and mechanical parts unfold, spin or slide into different configurations, so that mechanics of the process are effectively obscured in plain view; similarly the other robot transformations going on around Optimus and glimpsed in the background of the roving frame are only legible in terms of their general movement, not their detail."[69] While we are left with what Bould calls a "powerful fantasy of mutability,"[70] we receive at the same time a merely vague impression of change, a general sense of agitation replacing any detailed understanding of how these machines reassemble their mechanic bodies from one shape into another: *that* bodies morph from one form into another matters more for Bay's aesthetic than exactly *how* they do it, or whether this "how" in any way follows the principles of physics and engineering, however imaginary they may be.

Lugo is certainly no Optimus Prime. The latter's magnanimous rhetoric of leadership, of selfless service, of epic grandeur and benevolent paternalism, has no equivalent in the bodybuilder's compensatory postures of arrested development, his transformation of the American dream into a steroid fantasy. Lugo is driven by nagging feelings of economic disenfranchisement, a monstrous return of neoliberalism's repressed. Unable to understand that motivational resources and ceaseless self-management alone do not provide economic success in the face of the strictures of late-capitalist inequality, he turns to criminal activity to extend his personal boundaries and cash in the putative claims of his muscular work ethic. Optimus Prime, on the other hand, though of course an expert in physical transformation and self-armoring as well, sees the world from the other end of the spectrum. Nothing he ever does is done for the sole benefit of himself nor evaluated within an investment/profit matrix. His ethics are grounded not in visions of unconditional individualism and self-fulfillment but of sociability, self-denial, and sacrifice, the majestic "We" afforded by those whose authority at the top of the social pyramid is beyond question.

Despite such categorical differences, it is difficult to deny that Lugo attracts more attention in *Pain & Gain* and monopolizes more authority over the film's narrative process than it would be reasonable to expect. His schemes and deeds are clearly appalling, his rhetoric of fitness presented as the pathological underside of the neoliberal ideology of self-empowerment. Still, *Pain & Gain* certainly manages to make the viewer feel for and feel with Lugo, to see him as a victim of his own monstrous belief system, and hence to some degree to identify with him, fear for him, feel moved by his movements and efforts to escape capture. This could quickly be attributed to Bay's casting, using an actor who is known for tough and heroically individualist roles but rarely immoral or malicious ones. Another reason could be seen in the fact that in trying to infuse dark satire with certain elements of comedy, the director short-circuited incompatible generic dynamics, thus creating a protagonist who is more likable and less resistible than he should be.

The final reason, however, might be both more simple and more complex than these. Bay's cinema as a whole is a cinema of ceaseless motion, of transformative movement. Stillness has no place in his aesthetic. It fails the imperatives of dynamic cinematography and editing, and it betrays what, in Bay's view, defines humans (and machines) as moral agents, as being endowed with life and value. Lugo, like Optimus Prime, is a paragon of motion, an analogy and extension in the pro-filmic world of what Bay's cinema is all about. He carries the film as much as the film carries him, one body propelling and being propelled by another. However abhorrent its translation into economic practice and moral thought may be, the building of muscular bodies in Bay's films does the same work for them as the transformation of Autobot warriors from one vehicular shape into another. It puts cameras (physical or virtual) into motion and endows them with legitimacy. As if trying to live up to what Optimus Prime embodies, Lugo approaches his own body as a medium, malleable matter that simultaneously defines our being in the world and can be subjected to the transformative will of human consciousness. Fitness work reveals the essence of one's nature as something that can be shaped and reshaped in the course of time, as something antithetic to pause, stillness, and standstill. And in this it does what Optimus Prime and other (more positive) heroes of Bay's cinema do with seemingly irresistible force at all times as well: breathe life into what according to Bay is the most elemental task of motion pictures—namely, to show pictures in motion.

Lugo's at once Nietzschean and neoliberal philosophy of fitness goes hand in hand with his utter disregard of dead bodies. In one of *Pain & Gain*'s most distressing sequences, two dead bodies are chain-sawed into pieces and later barbequed to cover up collateral damage. The scene is meant to showcase Lugo's ruthless goal orientation while at the same time offering some comic relief for viewers who are unsure about how to fit Lugo into the matrix of Bay's world in general. All things told, however, there is very little to laugh about in this sequence, and any effort to expose, in a mode typical of a satire, Lugo's vices and intellectual limitations fires backward as well. The dead here are dead and done with. Mere corpses. De-animated, they lose any possible meaning not simply for Lugo and his team but for Bay himself as well. Dead bodies in film, Lesley Stern has written in a different context, have the ability to interrupt cinematic temporality; they pause the flow of images and temporarily fill screen space with a slowed-down sense of time, a certain sense of stillness, thus opening a space for reflection.[71] Stern's dead haunt Michael Bay's cinema at all times, for stillness is what his characters as much as his images themselves fear most. For Bay, dead bodies are dead matter. They no longer afford what drives his films take by take—namely, the promise of never-ending movement and agential transformation. In fact, Bay's dead bodies forfeit what his protagonists and Autobots have in common. They no longer serve as media, as tools of being in and acting on the world, and as such they define a limit to, and possibly even undermine, Bay's philosophy of total mediatization and ceaseless self-management. As if dying once were not enough, the dead must be killed over and over again so as to prevent the danger of empty time, of us merely contemplating the present without participating in its infinite mutability. They must be further mutilated to ensure that the past does not haunt or slow down future presents with uncomfortable claims and obligations.

Bay's Planets

The image of dead or fully instrumentalized matter, writes Jane Bennett,

> feeds human hubris and our earth-destroying fantasies of conquest and consumption. It does so by preventing us from detecting (seeing, hearing, smelling, tasting, feeling) a fuller range of the nonhuman powers circulating around and within human bodies. These material powers, which can aid or destroy, enrich or disable, ennoble or degrade us, in any case call for our attentiveness, or even "respect" (provided that the term be stretched beyond its Kantian sense). The figure of an intrinsically inanimate matter may be one of the impediments to the emergence of more ecological and more materially sustainable modes of production and consumption.[72]

Pain & Gain shows little patience for exploring the nonhuman in the human, let alone tuning into the vibrancy and vitality of matter not controlled by neoliberal visions of self-perfection, of fitness, of instrumentalizing matter for the sake of individual benefit and competitive expansion. Some of Bay's other work, however, reveals a much more pronounced awareness of the recalcitrance of things, the incommensurable strangeness of matter, be it human and man-made or not. It grants vitality, agency, and vibrancy to what is typically considered inanimate materiality, reveals some curiosity about what nonhuman objects can do, and in the process asks human protagonists—rather than to achieve full control over what eschews their understanding—to learn how to adapt to the shared materiality of all things, to tune into the vibrancy of all matter.

Don't worry: this will not turn into an outlandish suggestion to read Michael Bay as a twenty-first-century advocate of flower power. Instead it is meant to ask whether Bay's respect for and attentiveness to the agential powers of matter and the nonhuman should make us revise the hopes new materialists have come to attach to the agency of things. The film to explore this argument is *Armageddon*, Bay's first foray into science fiction, produced for $140 million, released as a summer blockbuster, and returning more than $550 million at the box office worldwide. Set in the present, *Armageddon* tells the story of a massive meteor shower taking aim at planet Earth and initially destroying various locations in the United States and elsewhere. NASA decides to send Harry Stamper (Bruce Willis), an experienced and rugged deep-sea oil driller, together with his rather unconventional team of social outcasts, into space in order to land with two special shuttles on the main and most threatening comet (the size of Texas), drill a deep hole into its surface, place and trigger a nuclear bomb, derail the comet's course, and in the process save Earth from replaying what, as detailed in the film's opening, happened sixty-five million years once before—namely, the massive extinction of life on Earth when an asteroid six miles in diameter struck the Yucatan Peninsula. Some of the crew die in the course of events when one of the shuttles crashes into the meteor, and most of the drilling, encountering materials unknown to Earth-bound humans, turns out to be much more difficult than expected. During the climactic finale, Stamper stays behind to launch the nuclear bomb whose triggering device had been damaged earlier. He sacrifices his life not only to make Earth live but also to enable the reunion of his daughter, Grace (Liv Tyler), with his most talented team member, A. J. Frost (Ben Affleck), and thus to pass on the baton of parental care to his future and posthumous son-in-law.

A Jerry Bruckheimer production, *Armageddon* was Bay's most expensive, most special effect–driven, most star-studded feature up to then. It was also his loudest picture, both acoustically and visually. Its action sequences, in particular the ones set on the asteroid, do everything at Bay's disposal (circa 1998) to extend the protagonists' physical activities, pain, trauma, disorientation, chaos, struggle, sacrifice, and victory to the viewer's sensory perception. As Bay described it in an interview: "In terms of the action scenes, I want the audience to feel like they're inside of it. That they are living it, and not just watching it from afar. I like putting the audience at privileged angles, where they're feeling it, rather than just watching it unfold in front of them. So I do try to create chaos with the action."[73] Whatever rumbles on-screen is to make the viewer rumble as well. Although a few decades after the film's release, the film's special effects may no longer persuade viewers that they live what they see, the camera's ongoing shaking and trembling, its refusal to provide steady views of the events, as well as the soundtrack's layering of unheard noises and reverberations continue to succeed in making the viewer feel the action on-screen at a visceral and somatic level, as if their chairs were strapped to the shuttles, the rovers, the drilling machineries themselves.

Throughout the asteroid sequence we see as little as Stamper's crew is able to see. Shrill clamor, produced by the asteroid's flight through space as much as Stamper's apparatus, assaults our ears no less than it seems to affect Stamper's men, navigating what is a categorically inhospitable environment. In the moments leading up to the climactic detonation scene, however, a certain shift in tone and atmosphere is noticeable. Stamper, described by A. J. as someone not known to fail, succeeds in pushing the trigger in the end, because he understands himself as being part of the very (high-speed) milieu he is set to destroy (fig. 16). In the moment immediately preceding their destruction, asteroid and human are shown as resonating with each other, the former's vibrating matter extending in and through the latter's body, the drilling expert's hand able to grasp the triggering device because his senses have adapted to the fact that the meteor seems to have its own logic, will, and determined path, its own agency. Similar to how Bay wants his audience to be "inside" the action of his films by allowing a film's sights and sounds to vibrate through the viewer's body, Stamper no longer experiences the asteroid's vibrations as fundamentally antagonistic to the motions of his own body.

Figure 16: Vibrant matter. *Armageddon* (1998) |

One of the last shots from Stamper's point of view shows parts of the asteroid framing the sight of planet Earth in the far distance, providing a brief moment of narrative delay and visual pause—as if the asteroid has become an extension of Stamper's own organs of perception and he has no more reason to sense the asteroid's speed as speed, because it has become part of his somatic system of reference, a self-sustained ecosystem of sensory resonance and reciprocity.

"Each human," writes Jane Bennett, "is a heterogeneous compound of wonderfully vibrant, dangerously vibrant, matter. If matter itself is lively, then not only is the difference between subjects and objects minimized, but the status of the shared materiality of all things is elevated. All bodies become more than mere objects, as the thing-powers of resistance and protean agency are brought into sharper relief."[74] In the climactic detonation scene of *Armageddon*, we experience Stamper as at once wonderfully and dangerously vibrant, a vibrancy shared with the "thing-power" of the asteroid, its recalcitrance and obstinacy, its power to speak in its own voice, its agency. What it takes to blow up and derail the comet, and hence to prevent a replay of what extinguished life on spaceship Earth once before, is to liquefy the boundary between subject and object. It is to recognize the fact that even the most foreign matter vibrates, has a life of its own, is more than a mere and mute object. In spite of all his uncontrolled emotions, once a model of Enlightenment reason who is set to approach and instrumentalize the natural world as a mere resource of human exploits and superiority, by the end of *Armageddon* Stamper emerges as a new materialist who in the very moment of destroying his surrounds recognizes the very connectedness of all things. His last moments bear testimony to the fact that human history is part of a much larger history, and that the world of material objects, in all their alienness, may be endowed with their own views of things, their own (alien) phenomenology.[75]

For Stamper, in order to destroy the asteroid, you have to learn how to vibrate with it. To save humanity from the willfulness of the material world, you have to discover your own materiality, become object yourself, and relinquish visions of absolute human sovereignty. Yet, this being a Michael Bay film rather than a Greenpeace documentary, we might be well-advised to turn this final insight on its head as well and ask whether in Bay's vision of world cinema, to vibrate with the world and resonate with the different materialities around us is to unleash destructive powers, and whether for Stamper to recognize that matter matters becomes possible only in its very moment of extinction. Though even at Wesleyan Bay is unlikely to have read his work, philosopher Martin Heidegger might be helpful to untangle this issue. In his essay concerning the question of technology, Heidegger famously quoted the German poet Friedrich Hölderlin: "But where danger is, grows / The saving power also."[76]

Although essential to revealing the essence of human nature and being in the world, the particular nature of modern technology and media for Heidegger had the dangerous capacity to conceal Being from us. Reducing nature to a mere resource, a standing reserve, Heidegger's technology in the modern age operated as a mere *Gestell*, a mechanism enframing rather than revealing the nature of things, including the thingness of the human body. But not all was lost: the very process that occluded Being also provided what it takes to overcome it. It allows us to play out the forces of concealment against themselves and recognize the power of technology as a medium to reveal the truth of Being, of what it means to be human under modern conditions. Modern technology's true threat is not in the machines, in how apparatus may destroy existing conditions of life. It is in how it may prevent humans from understanding their own existence, the primal truth of what it means to be human, even though technology—properly understood—is nothing other but a means, a medium, to reveal "the shining-forth and holding-sway of truth."[77]

Bay's planetary cinema out-Heideggers the German philosopher at his own game. Moments of danger allow Bay's protagonists not simply to prevent the complete ruin of objects and lives but also to bring the essence of things into genuine appearing. Danger empowers his heroes to use technologies—weapons, bombs, vehicles, spaceships—as means and media to recalibrate their relation to matter. As Heidegger would put, danger in Bay's films fetches into essence that all matter vibrates, that the world of things may be animated and have its own claims, and that human affairs may be only one chapter within a much larger story of animation and thing-powers. But even though his films often think of things human in planetary dimensions and of technology as a medium to reveal the resonant connectedness of all matter, it would gravely miss the point to consider the whole of Bay's cinema as being a cinema of ecological and materialist sensibilities, a cinema envisioning a future in which we may rediscover resonances between the human and the nonhuman as the saving powers in the face of our environmental catastrophes of the present.

Whether the focus is on the matter of architecture, of human flesh, or of galactic bodies, Bay's cinema eagerly wants to remind the viewer that, amid our age of digital abstractions and ever increasing dematerialization, the materiality of things continues to matter, precisely because they can be seen and experienced as media, as a scaffold for our entire being in the world. Moreover, as the epic framing of the *Transformers* franchise and of films such as *Armageddon* indicates, Bay's stories, sounds, and images certainly tend to envisage human affairs from a nonhuman vantage point, and to make us understand the extent to which histories that are hugely in excess of human willfulness shape the very parameters according to which we perceive, sense, and understand them. All things told, however, whatever smacks of post-humanist materialism in Bay's films is purchased at the very price of annihilating what might require saving. Bound to entertain his audiences at all cost with vibrating spectacles of danger and mayhem, Bay causes protagonists and viewers alike solely to resonate with matter that destroys or is presented in need of destruction. Even if this destructive impulse is carried out with imaginary special effects, there is therefore no way to understand Bay's enframing of matter, media, and Being as a utopian blueprint for materially sustainable modes of production and consumption. So much does his cinema rely on danger as a resource of thrill, speed, and box office returns that his action sequences consume the very saving powers they promise to generate.

Sound

Imagine that due to some bizarre twist of fate, we all found ourselves in a universe designed by Michael Bay—to live amid his heroes, in the face of whatever challenge they encounter, drawn into one rescue operation after another. Audiologists, it is clear, would have no shortage of possible patients in this world. For Bay's universe is a loud and noisy one, the aggressive sounds of firing guns, battling machines, collapsing infrastructures, splintering glass, spinning cars, and shrieking humans pressing hard against what healthy eardrums can tolerate for long without suffering major damage. Bay's world does not know of the pleasures of intimate sounds, let alone regenerative moments of silence. Similar to how dead bodies bear little meaning for Bay's protagonists, silence for them simply denotes the absence of action and commotion, a state of standstill in which bodies fail to display their full potential and minds cannot successfully attend to relevant matters, tasks, and missions. Silence is bland, a vortex of nonexistence. It is the ground of primordial immobility against which

Bay's figures of action and movement gain their contours, their resolution, their attraction. Whether they are humans or machines, for Bay's heroes to reveal what they are best at and to actualize their innermost essences means to make noise and engage with noisy things. It is to navigate contexts that assault the ear, to act as if tympanic membranes did not exist. Noise, in Bay's films, is life. It is existence. It is movement. It is what motion pictures are all about. In Bay's world, tinnitus is the universal ground zero of acoustical perception. It's the veil through which people hear whatever they consider audible.

But then again, there is no need simply to imagine how it would sound and feel if we lived inside Bay's worlds. For the soundtracks of Bay's features, from the very moment their projection begins, are designed to provide experiences of rich spatial immersion, of seamless "in-ness." Bay's films hugely capitalize on sound's spherical rather than directional nature, its enveloping rather than perspectival qualities. They provide complex textures and multilayered blankets of sound to engage the viewer's perception from all sides, and they effectively fold the viewer sensorially into the action. Although critics typically comment on the speed of Bay's images, his sounds are at least as important to cause the viewer to attend to the spectacle on-screen, at once amplifying and, as we will see in a moment, compensating for certain deficits of high-velocity visibility. True to Bay's early career in the making of music videos, the acoustical properties of his films play a crucial role in placing the viewer in a story's particular space and imprinting the pace and rhythm of narrative time onto our sensory perception, our bodily sense of time. Bay's heroes' noise is our noise. Their tinnitus is ours.

Classical Hollywood cinema (and cinema studies) often considered a film's soundtrack as secondary to its visual choreography. Nondiegetic music was at its best when it was setting emotions and providing narrative cues right below the viewer's threshold of active recognition. Film music relied on "unheard melodies,"[78] massaging the audience's feelings and stitching plot elements together without drawing awareness to themselves. Sound effects were largely a matter of postproduction, added to a feature once its images were in the can. The editing of dialogue scenes and voice-overs, though of course greatly important to drive a particular film forward, typically followed the exigencies of a film's particular look, the way images had been captured and cut according to dominant templates of rhythm and flow. Even though the term has not become a universal currency yet, postclassical cinema as we have come to know it over the last few decades has questioned and recalibrated some of these tenets. Musical soundtracks often stand on their own feet, with their intention to promote or be promoted by current hit songs. Sound effects, produced for complex surround projection situations, increasingly draw awareness to themselves as elements that lend depth and breadth to the fleeting images on-screen. "I regard sound as being very important, more essential than pictures," Iranian art house filmmaker Abbas Kiarostami once suggested, somewhat to the surprise of those who had celebrated the photographic compositions and painterly qualities of his cinema. "A two-dimensional flat image is all you can achieve with your camera, whatever you may do. It's the sound that gives depth as the third dimension to that image. Sound, in fact, makes up for this shortcoming of pictures. Compare architecture and painting. The former deals with space while all you have in painting is surface."[79]

Whether we think of Bay's films as efforts to continue, intensify, reframe, or displace the dogmas of classical narrative filmmaking, Bay's cinema in general, and his use of film music, dialogue, sound effects, and noise in particular, is certainly architectural through and through. Its function is much more complex than either to entertain the viewer with unheard melodies, set moods, and offer subliminal narrative cues, or to market popular music, inundate the audience with spectacular acoustical commotion, and explore unseen aspects of the moving image. Instead, its mission is to invite viewers to experience cinema as a spatial art form, and space as something inherently dynamic rather than static. Bay's sounds set up three-dimensional environments that contain and draw together all aspects of the filmic experience. They define a vivid ambience designed to be inhabited by (and to inhabit) the viewer's entire sensory perception, to be navigated by (and to navigate) the spectator's virtual movements through Bay's narratives and make such movements feel much less virtual than classical screen theory always wanted us to believe. Sound in Bay's films is essential not simply to identify relations in and of space but to dynamize our perception of spatial properties as well. It echoes how mobile subjects experience a cityscape as both a given setup for physical movements and a malleable structure activated by the subject's never fully predictable modes of seeing and moving through the world. Bay's sounds make us feel as if even the most hostile world is our world. They, like architecture, position and direct our senses in the world as much as they communicate the impression that the world responds to the perception of its users, that it requires our acts of perceiving to come into being in the first place.

Few filmmakers today are more committed than Michael Bay to the ideas that (1) seeing may no longer count as the most privileged channel of human sensory perception, and that (2) we would betray the rich possibilities of visual perception if we reduced our sense of seeing to the operations of the eye alone. To "see" a film, in Bay's universe, is to register a screening with one's entire sensorium and to experience the embodied nature of all perception; it is to partake of the extent to which we cannot uncouple the workings of the eye from our sense of touch, of the haptic, tactile, and kinesthetic. Contrary to those who may argue that tactile modes of looking in cinema remain metaphorical because we never really lay our hands on the image itself, Bay's use of sound largely figures as a medium to affect the viewer at a somatic level. As intricate as his visual choreography, Bay's sound designs are indeed devised to connect the movements of narrative action and the viewer's psychophysical receptors with the help of the physical vibration of sound waves. We may always see Bay's images at a distance regardless of how close their frantic editing suggests they be. But we have little choice but to feel Bay's sounds with our entire body, to experience the clamor of his films acting upon us and resonating through our flesh as if our skin directly touched the skin of the screen.

Richard Wagner's compositional methods, in their effort to fuse different tracks of artistic expression into one unified *Gesamtkunstwerk*, played a key role in the formation of the Hollywood soundtrack during the classic studio era of the 1930s. German and Austrian exile and émigré composers helped translate Wagner's musical idiom—his use of "endless" melody and leitmotif, his way of pitching music right below the volume of the human voice, his methods of using music to explore character motivation and illuminate their unconscious—into the affective language of film music, regardless of the fact that Wagner's thought and music had energized the very movement that had expelled these composers from central Europe.[80] What remained mostly forgotten in this complex and tragically ironic process of cultural transfer was that Wagner envisioned his total work of art as both an aesthetic and a political intervention to counteract what he considered the pathological separation of sensory perception in industrial modernity. Far from merely serving as a tool of musical seduction or, as the late Friedrich Nietzsche wanted to have it, as an incubator of sickness and depravity, Wagner's sounds were meant to overcome how modern society in Wagner's mythological view had fragmented the human sensorium. The function of good sound was no less than to restore what it would take to make humans whole again and allow them to resonate with the world.

It is difficult to imagine any of Bay's most ardent fans sitting through five hours of *Tristan and Isolde*, let alone exposing themselves to Wagner's *Ring of the Nibelung*, to be staged over at least eighteen hours during four consecutive evenings. But what sounds do in Bay's films to carry the drama, affect the viewer, and tie different sensory registers together might come much closer to Wagner's original vision than what any Hollywood composer in the early days of synchronized sound cinema ever envisioned. Mixed for advanced Dolby Surround Sound projection, be it Dolby 5.1 or 7.1 or Dolby Atmos, as in the case of *Transformers: Age of Extinction*, Bay's sounds define (post-)classical cinema as a sensual architecture that is able to reunite the splintered art forms of what Wagner called music, dance, and poetry (and what more contemporary audiences might consider sound, action, and dialogue). No matter how piercing their volumes, the acoustical properties of Bay's films are key to navigating the viewer through and beyond a modern age of distinct media so as to reintegrate our fragmented senses of seeing, hearing, touch, taste, and movement. Sound in Bay's films, as in Wagner's music, is as much product as it is process. It positions cinema as a work in progress, charged with the mission of recalibrating the audience's senses, moving the spectator beyond the sensory isolation of the everyday, and allowing the contemporary subject to experience perceptual synthesis as a promissory note for a non-alienated future. Sound reveals what exceeds the merely visible. It complicates character motivation, communicates what it may feel to be touched by the action, and, in so doing, renders tangible that Bay's dynamic universe is way too rich to be mapped with one sense alone.

Consider a very short sequence of events in the first *Transformers* film whose complexity and detail of design might easily be lost on anyone watching the film as it initially was meant to be experienced (fig. 17).

Figure 17: Groans and screams.
Transformers (2007)

Figure 17: *Continued* |

Here's what you can witness amid the unfolding street battle in downtown Los Angeles if you pause and delay the scene's frantic action with your remote control in hand: We start with Autobot Bumblebee handing the AllSpark—Bay's version of Wagner's ring of the Nibelung, an object too powerful to be possessed by anyone—to the film's human protagonist, Sam Witwicky (Shia LaBeouf). Bumblebee is known for his curious speech impediment, his being restricted to communicating solely through sampled radio transmissions. In this particular moment, however, when placing the mysterious cube in the care of his human ally, Bumblebee articulates a deep and somewhat extraterrestrial groan, a sound reverberating somewhere between the human and the robotic. Next, we briefly see Sam admiring the AllSpark before Decepticon Megatron enters the scene and transforms from a black pickup truck into his more familiar shape while propelled missiles fly by and buildings crumble left and right. As usual, Megatron's shapeshifting takes place as part of a speedy course of forward action, in mid-motion and mid-stride, as it were. It also involves an acrobatic rotational leap, at the end of which Megatron lands on his by then fully articulated shoulder, rolls over, and continues his destructive path by foot.

Little of this scene might really be noteworthy were it not for two more aspects. First is the sight of a woman crouching on the ground in a state of terror while Megatron, in his transformational rotation, flies right over her head. Presented in slow motion, the camera passes the woman from right to left while her head moves in the opposite direction so as to follow the path of Megatron above her and witness his landing to her left. Mixed into the strangely muted mechanical sounds of Megatron's transformation, of his making contact with the asphalt, and of the horizontal passing of various missiles is the woman's prolonged scream, her acoustical outburst of panic presented in audio slow motion. The second feature of note occurs when Megatron finally lands on his shoulder, his head upside down and slightly pushed to the side, his eyes directly facing and making contact with the screaming woman's eyes. What we hear—blended into the scream and the noise of metal hitting asphalt—is another groan. It is as astonishing and uncanny as Bumblebee's earlier one, yet this time it originates from the Decepticon warrior right before he resumes his destructive thrust and before the musical soundtrack kicks in again to add fuel to the fire of his mayhem.

Lasting no longer than thirty seconds, the scene in question is packed with visual and acoustical information. It would take many pages to identify each of its elements in appropriate detail and to untangle the different trajectories of action and its dense layers of attraction. What primarily matters for our context here, however, is how Bay incorporates mechanical and human, industrial and organic noises into one highly dynamic soundscape, whose vibrations and resonances will not be lost on the viewer even if this viewer will be unable to describe exactly what he or she saw. Far from simply supplementing the visible, sound here—in all of its different registers—drives the image, sets the pace for the action, makes things legible, and channels the viewer's affects. More specifically, the film's acoustical properties provide signs of psychological depth, interpretative possibility, and semantic complexity where we might expect them the least. Shared by both Bumblebee and Megatron, the audible groan does not simply define both Transformers as existing somewhere in between the mechanical and organic; it also suggests surprising continuities between what, from the outside, appears to be a clear-cut opposition of good and evil. Autobots and Decepticons, we may conclude, have more in common than what their epic history of enmity at first communicates. And yet, because Bumblebee's and Megatron's groans resound in response to very different triggers and micro-situations, Bay's sound design simultaneously sets limits to any effort to fully understand the affective and expressive registers of these animated machines. Outwardly inviting the viewer to explore the psychological disposition of these beings, and hence to do what Wagner's use of musical leitmotifs was designed to do in the mid-nineteenth century, Bay's soundtrack leaves little doubt that humans fail to read the nonhuman—that Transformers, no matter how human they may act at certain junctures, involve forms of matter and agency that exceed human understanding. Although much of this will remain unnoticed by the casual viewer, Bay's sounds thus at once mobilize and place under erasure Wagner's musical effort to reveal the work and language of the unconscious. Rather than expose what we do not know, Bay's groans in LA unsettle any desire to assimilate the other, the unknown, and the nonhuman to the templates of human interpretative knowledge. All we know is that we can never really know what makes Transformers moan like humans.

But do we understand any better what makes humans tick? There can be no doubt about the cause of the woman's prolonged scream in this scene. She has good reason to shriek in horror, threatened to death by what she sees and senses all around her. We certainly feel with her and for her; it requires no effort to read her and the entire situation to understand what triggers her emotional response. Nevertheless, Bay's use of slow-motion audio to express and communicate her panic is somewhat puzzling, or, as seasoned Brechtians would say, estranging.

When trying to decelerate recorded sounds for the sake of creative experimentation in the 1960s, minimalist composers quickly discovered that any effort to slow down the audible would unfavorably lower and distort a sound's pitch.[81] Prior to digital frequency correction, to slow down sound was simply to engineer a different sound. Unlike slow-motion photography's ability to render visible what escapes ordinary perception, slow-motion sound had no real capacity to expose something new or in detail about the structural composition of a particular sound. It merely displaced this sound for another sound, one that struck the ear as strange and incommensurable. Though digital technologies now allow sound engineers to slow down acoustical figures without lowering their pitch, slow-motion sound remains much of an oddity. Iconic action sequences—think of the famous "bullet time" sequence in *The Matrix* (1999), think of various slow-motion inserts in Bay's work ever since *The Rock*—typically set decelerated images against steady, fast-paced musical beats so as not to irritate their viewers with perceived clashes of different speeds and temporalities. Slow-motion images persist as a staple in twenty-first-century cinema to intensify drama, action, human agency, and agony. Slow-motion sound, on the other hand, continues to be perceived as so special an effect that it produces counterproductive affects and non-empathetic distance among the audience.

This, one might want to argue, is exactly what happens when Bay records the scream of the panicked woman during Megatron's transformational leap in slow motion. Bay's camera moves around her from an extreme low angle so that we can see the rotating gestalt of Megatron flying above her, and the soundtrack blocks out some of the other ambient noises (of which there could be plenty) so that we can fully take in the woman's extended squeal. Although digital interventions have elevated the pitch of her voice to expectable levels, her scream nevertheless sounds unmistakably manufactured, void of what typically characterizes the voice as the most immediate organ of human expressiveness. Due to the impact of slow motion, it sounds both mechanic and organic, technologically engineered and embodied. It signifies an outcry of the human yet also echoes the effects of her robotic and destructive environment, as if her body and voice had secretly assimilated already to all that is non- and antihuman around her, as if survival of the human depended on a human's ability to become half machine first. If Bumblebee, in this installment of the *Transformers* franchise, is able to communicate solely by sampling words gathered from car radios and hence by situating himself as a ventriloquist's dummy, Bay's soundtrack profiles the woman not as the human verso to the film's recto of ubiquitous technology but as a hybrid being that suspends the very boundary between dummy and ventriloquist. She speaks by being spoken. She screams the echoes of technological violence. Her voice is as much hers at it belongs to the machines that reign over the streets of LA and, by extension, the operations of Bay's cinema.

The shot featuring the woman's squeal of terror lasts twelve seconds (which for devoted Bay viewers might approximate eternity). Few audience members will recall its presence given the visual and acoustical frenzy both preceding and succeeding this take. In any event, the shot abounds with ontological conundrums and metaphysical subtleties. Most importantly, it features what should be understood as highly ambiguous echoes of how Wagner sought to relate image and sound, drama and the acoustical. On the one hand, the scene seemingly integrates the woman's scream into the multilayered musical and nonmusical soundtrack of the film. Music with other means, in this instance the woman's hybrid sounds—similar to the ambitions of Wagner's compositional techniques—reveal emotional complexities hidden beneath the merely visible. They tap into and put into action the visual unconscious and thereby render much more complex and ambivalent what is designed to meet the eye.

On the other hand, however, to the extent to which Bay's soundtrack presents the woman as both dummy and ventriloquist, as body and machine, it casts into question what Wagner's musical techniques were all about—namely, to expose the psychological depth and mysterious animation of human interiority. What Bay's sounds of the woman reveal is nothing less than that there is no longer much to reveal at all about the human. What we hear is that the human as such—as a being that is being spoken and screamed—no longer exists; that human psychology in an age of ubiquitous machines and technologies has become a thing of the past; that human interiority is a mere effect of highly mediated environments, a medium rather than an essence. All things told, what we witness in these twelve seconds is nothing less than Bay beating Wagner at his own game, out-Wagnering the master. If Wagner hoped, with the help of music, to redeem the human from the burden of modern machines, Bay resorts to Wagnerian techniques to flee into an age in which stable boundaries between humans and machines have all but disappeared.

It should come as little surprise, then, that Bay's sounds inhabit a crossroad between innovation and tradition that is as least as ambiguous as Wagner's own musical language, whose romantic quest for perceptual synthesis and sensory reintegration prepared the ground for modernist forays into dissonance and foiled tonal resolution. Sound designers and engineers who worked on *Transformers: Dark of the Moon* have reported the extent to which, in their effort to push the film's soundtrack to new levels, they "talked about how we take organic sounds and twist them into the electronics, and conversely how we take electronic sounds and sort of twist them into the organic world."[82]

We may often think, rightly, of Bay's soundtracks as continuous assaults on the human ear, richly layered yet ultimately indistinguishable blankets of noise, so dynamic in nature that no listener has time to decode what he or she just heard. However, we should not lose sight of the fact that these soundtracks often result from many human hours of creative experimentation and laboratory-like exploration, that they involve the work of many a tinkerer and digital geek for whom the audible is a rich field, not just of playing tricks on the audience but of systematic research and accidental discovery. Therefore, while Bay himself is mostly a winner of the Golden Raspberry Award for worst director and worst picture, his sound crews have repeatedly been nominated for Academy Awards, recognized for their diligent and pioneering efforts to push sound to new frontiers. When in *Transformers: Dark of the Moon* airborne battleships, robots, and human warriors engage one another on the streets of Chicago to fight over the use of the so-called Pillars, what audience members hear mixed into the noise blasting from the theater's surround systems might as well be the sounds of screwdrivers scratching the strings of electric guitars, or pieces of dry ice resonating within metallic echo chambers. What we hear when the action is at its most pounding is the sound of Optimus Prime's guns playing the eighth and sixteenth notes of the orchestral soundtrack, thus blurring the boundary between the diegetic and the nondiegetic as much as between the visible and the audible.

Sound in Bay's films is rarely what it seems to be at face value. In many cases it produces a complex field of semantic ambiguities, sensory crossovers, and unexpected inversions. Few people may be willing to make and sustain the experiment, but to watch a Michael Bay film with your eyes wide shut and your ears wide open to the opulent fabrics of acoustical material may produce some unexpected wonders—no less wondrous perhaps than what might happen if you allowed Wagner's bombastic Germanic myths to recede into the background and simply focused your listening on the weaving and unweaving of his musical language. In the second act of Wagner's *Die Meistersinger von Nürnberg*, Hans Sachs muses about Walther's unsettling effort to sing a prize song—that is to say, the curious way that Walther's youthful modernity echoes and reveals the presumed language of nature: "It sounded so old, and yet it was so new." Bay's soundtracks are similar to Walther's "Morgenlich leuchtend im rosigen Schein" (Glowing in the rosy light of morning) in that they rely on advanced techniques to produce impressions of epic and seemingly ahistorical grandeur as much as they mobilize the organic and presumably timeless to signify the technological gadgets of the future. Even when sound in Bay's films is meant to sound old, it may be of experimental novelty, and whatever may strike the ear as utterly novel may in fact be deeply familiar. Wagner's shoemaker and poet Hans Sachs would have a field day if we resurrected him from his dual grave in sixteenth-century Nuremberg and nineteenth-century Bayreuth and placed him amid a theatrical screening of Bay's *Transformers: Dark of the Moon*.

But to think of Bay's use of sound as a quasi-Wagnerian strategy of rendering the image more complex, to unlock or stockpile layers of possible meaning in excess of the visible and its frantic rate of action is of course to address not even half the story of how the audible in Bay's cinema is designed to work on the viewer. What is missing from this story is how Bay's sounds, due in particular to the options of surround technology and multitrack digital sound mixing, purposefully engineer perceptions of continuity that Bay's frantic images themselves no longer necessarily afford. According to Bruce Isaacs's poignant analysis, "Sequences are often cut so frenetically as to disorient the spectator within the visual and sonic field. Image relations often deliberately break continuity, fragmenting a hermetic field into a series of abstractly related parts. In action scenes, Bay will often break several of the basic rules of spatio-temporal continuity, such as cutting 'across the line,' or cutting through unmotivated framing (*mise en scène*)."[83]

Though mixed no less for visceral effect than for signification, Bay's sounds often relate and re-bond what his feverish visual editing shows as discontinuous. Loud, noisy, chaotic, and at times seemingly undifferentiated, they are always assembled and designed as elements of a vibrant soundscape, meant to envelop the viewer's perception, as part of a sound field placing us in the action on-screen and relating us to it even if—or, better, precisely because—the dynamic elements of the visual field forbid orientation and perceptual unity. Sound in Bay's films is therefore much more than a mere attribute of the visible, a mechanism to reveal what escapes the movements of the eye. Instead, it conjures a unified space and offers auditory points of view, no matter how messy the visual information might be. It details a dynamic field of audible attractions that are powerful enough to incorporate and assimilate what initially seems to defy locality, clarity, and proper place. Individual sequences may wildly combine sounds coming from the diegetic or the nondiegetic, from areas on- or off-frame, from the acousmatic or the embodied. Although the images in the film are fragmented and deeply disorienting, the soundtrack, in contrast, provides a continuous flow, a container of acoustical stimulation integrating different sensory input for the viewer. Never approached in sheer isolation from one another, Bay's sounds thus do not simply counterbalance visual incoherence. They anchor the visible in its very fragmentation, release the image from providing readability at all costs, and thus precisely redefine what it might mean to speak of continuity in cinema today.

Consider the so-called Haitian shootout scene in *Bad Boys II*, in which detectives Lowrey and Burnett enter the labyrinthine house of a

Haitian gang involved in drug trafficking between Miami, Amsterdam, and Cuba (fig. 18). What ensues is a wild gunfight captured with at least equally wild camera movements and editing strategies. Bruce Bennett describes the scene's visual composition as follows: "While Mike and Marcus are in one room and the gang members are in the next, both sides shooting and shouting through holes in the dividing wall and the connecting doorways, the camera tracks back and forth between the two rooms tracing five complete circles. This is not presented as a single shot since it is interrupted with close-ups and medium shots of the actors yelling and firing, but nevertheless, and in spite of the furious action, the mobile point-of-view of the circling camera grabs our attention."[84] Similar to the scene from *Transformers* discussed earlier, it would take many more pages to cover each and every aspect of what unfolds in front of our eyes and batters our eardrums during this shootout sequence. One could and perhaps should mention the use of mirrors to calculate shot trajectories to be taken in the absence of clear sight; the firing of bullets through holes in walls and doors, including those that take direct aim at peeking eyes; the drugged-out craze of some of the participants as they experience their own death as life's most thrilling pleasure; the role of bathrooms and toilet bowls as sites providing temporary shelter only to be completely pierced by projectiles in the process. But even without including additional elements, there can be little doubt that Bay indeed uses the scene's approximately five minutes of screen time as a viable textbook case of how to grab the viewer's attention, and even more so, of how to immerse the spectator in the action in the relative absence of what in classical Hollywood cinema would have provided a sense of spatial contiguity and coherence.

Even though Bay's camera circles through various rooms of the house and thus indicates the positions of the combatants in their relation to one another, the velocity of its movements as much as the use of sudden cutaways and varying filming speeds thwarts any effort to anchor each participant properly in space, let alone render the house's architectural layout—the scene's spatial infrastructure—in any way legible. On the other hand, Bay's use of sound in this sequence does not simply compensate for what his images may no longer accomplish; it also articulates a zone of audible attractions—a dynamic acoustical environment—that emancipates his cinematography and editing from any overt need to tie

Figure 18: Haitian shootout. *Bad Boys II* (2003) |

things logically together. The affordances of surround sound here offer a perceptual framework that enables Bay's images to play. To be sure, what we mostly hear are gunshots that are as volatile and possibly disorienting in nature as the succession of images on-screen—that is, Bay's post-representational show of movement, light, color, and discontinuous cutting. Yet what his sounds, which are deliberately choreographed for a surround theatrical or domestic viewing situation, do in this sequence is to create a dense spatial fabric, a self-enclosed sonic environment, integrating what at the visual level alone would seem to defy integration and orientation. Screaming voices penetrate the walls of the house long before bullets shred them into pieces. Bits and pieces of dialogue connect the two police protagonists while Bay's cinematography, in its typical refusal of establishing and reframing shots, provides little clues about their location relative to each other. The resonance of human words and firing guns offers some sense of horizontal levelness even when

Figure 18: *Continued* |

the camera enjoys the freedom and thrill of extremely canted angles or suddenly cuts to extreme close-ups. Eventually the beats of nondiegetic electronic music blend into the mechanical thuds of weaponry as if trying to add steady rhythm, direction, and spatial totality to the frenzy shootout that is visible on-screen. Systematically exploring and utilizing the capacity of surround sound to construct virtual spaces that feel no less than real, Bay's Haitian shootout sequence—contrary to the opinions of all of those who claim that his visual style tends to unmoor physical action from concrete coordinates—thus provides a very clear sense of place, location, and direction. You may best recognize this, though, if you simply close your eyes and follow the film's acoustical clues. Bay's sounds are loud, raucous, piercing, at times overwhelming. But they are also the product of rigorous calculation and highly proficient engineering, defining conclusive environments for the action that enable the camera to do its own thing and that invite us to care much less for the coherence of Bay's images than image-centered viewers, critics, and scholars of cinema are often willing to admit.

"I love musicals," Bay has remarked. "When you talk about filmmaking, that was the first type of movie to really exploit film as a medium. Musicals give the viewer privileged angles, they break the walls and do a lot of unorthodox things."[85] No one is likely to see direct lines of influence between *West Side Story* (1961, dir. Robert Wise and Jerome Robbins) or *The Sound of Music* (1965, dir. Robert Wise) and Bay's cinema of excess in general; nor will they recognize how action sequences such as the one in *Bad Boys II* treat images as if they were music with other means and make sound drive, amplify, and contain the frenzy of the visible. The social topographies of Bay's twenty-first century are far too complex to be broken down into a drama about two gangs simply opposing each other, let alone one about how love—no matter how deadly—can point us toward redemption. And nothing in Bay's films of what fascinates us about contemporary Miami, its glitz, its ethnic hybridity, its post-monolingualism, its blend of wealth and crime, bears any resemblance to what fascinated American viewers about the Austrian Alps in the 1960s, about solid family values trumping Nazi politics. But breaking walls and doing unorthodox things *Bad Boys II* certainly does, in direct continuation of how the classical Hollywood musical often allowed song and dance to disrupt narrative continuity and insert moments of cinematic self-reflexivity.

During its quintuple spin through the Haitian hideout, each time Bay's camera moves through holes in walls or window panes to jump the classical axis and transport the viewer into the opponents' spaces, we hear a brief whizzing noise—a sound that is not present, of course, to the protagonists in the shootout. Bay's whoosh features and applauds the camera's extraordinary agility in this scene, its speed as much as its capacity to defy architectural restrictions. As importantly, this sound indexes a volatile breaking down of how classical Hollywood cinema constructed its walls of illusionism, destabilizing the boundary between the diegetic and the nondiegetic. It profiles the camera not as an invisible recording device that does not belong to the action's diegetic space but as a willful agent that is seemingly present amid, and contributes to, the very action it captures. Similar to how blood in contemporary action cinema often splatters onto the lens of the camera and thereby reminds us of its very presence, Bay's whizzing noise locates the camera as an active participant in the very space of the action, as a medium defying gravity, breaking walls, and precisely thus energizing what we see.

What might be unorthodox about this, however, is not that, in blurring the line between the diegetic and the nondiegetic, Bay would subscribe to some kind of self-reflexive criticality, exposing the work that cinema does to produce illusion, identification, and affective responses in the viewer. What is unorthodox, instead, is the fact that Bay's whizz equates action with perception itself, that it uses the acoustical blurring of the diegetic and the nondiegetic as a means to intensify our sense of continuity, and that in so doing it effectively terminates critical orthodoxies that continue to consider directorial gestures of breaking the wall as entry points for reflexive acts of viewing film, of critical estrangement. In Bay's world the Brechtian legacy of alienation and self-reflexivity no longer has any bearing. To break the wall is by no means to situate the viewer as an emancipated one. Instead it is to consolidate the extent to which our world of ubiquitous media no longer knows of any outside at all. Rather than to crack open the filmic text and ask viewers to change the real, Bay's collapsing of the diegetic and nondiegetic echoes historical dynamics that have come to define the social and the political as cinema—as musicals—with other means, as spectacles that are fully commensurable with contemporary cinema's mode of producing and monetizing mobile perceptions and perceptions of mobility.

In the burgeoning field of sound art studies, the audible has recently emerged as a privileged category to contest Western hierarchies of the senses and their implication in dominant constructions of power, identity, and action. Although some scholars rightly warn us not to consider sound's immersive, affective, and spherical qualities as a biological and quasi-theological given,[86] many others think of our sense of hearing as a potent entry to challenge the humanist subject and its narcissist fantasies of control and self-management.[87] Unlike vision, they argue, sound emphasizes the physical connectedness of all things, the fact that all things, including our bodies, vibrate and may be experienced as sound-producing entities. Rather than reinforcing the cold mastery of the eye, audibility is all about synchronizing the rhythm of objects with the rhythms of the perceiver; it is about how perceiver and perceived constitute each other in reciprocal events of resonance. Whereas traditional Western concepts of being in the world have typically claimed that matter is passive and life is radically different from matter, sonic materialists and object-oriented ontologists today think of sound as a medium to reconstruct the relationship between life and matter, mind and embodiment, animation and objecthood. Sound does not know of mute, dumb, and passive objects in the world. It only knows of the excitation of resonant materials, often independent of representation and signification. If the idea of intrinsically inanimate matter has historically impeded the emergence of more sustainable modes of production and consumption, a renewed stress on the acoustical could have no less than the capacity to make us think of the world as "a world filled not with ontologically distinct categories of beings (subjects and objects) but with variously composed materialities that form confederations."[88] It can help us to construct future worlds in which human bodies and nonhuman forces can reverberate with each other and invite the modern subject to open up to what exceeds the human and to experience the capacity of things, of matter, to act upon and resonate through the human.

There is no doubt that the recent writings of sonic materialists, speculative realists, and object-oriented audiophiles do not belong to Michael Bay's reading list. They do not really need to, though. For Bay knows a thing or two himself about how to make matter vibrate, about how vibration as audible sound may resonate through the viewer's body. Much of what we hear in Bay's soundtracks is beyond representation and signification: it is primarily there as a source of excitation, as a medium to synchronize the rhythms of the action on-screen with the rhythms of the audience. It leads us to form confederations with the materialities and physical actions displayed in the visual field. It lends the action a three-dimensional, spherical, and immersive extension in the auditorium, and it thus compels the viewer to abandon stances of subjective distance and control and instead experience the world as one of post-humanist reverberations. Image-centered film criticism misses some of Bay's most effective techniques of redefining cinema as a visceral event, as a skin that is not just worn on the body but that reconfigures the very way this body places itself, and allows itself to be placed, in the world. Sound matters to Bay as rarely in the work of other filmmakers before. It makes matter *matter*.

And yet, inasmuch as Bay's proficient choreography of sound in space produces vibrant ecologies of resonance, it also indicates the extent to which we may want to meet recent academic views about sound's productive ability to destabilize the humanist subject with some skepticism. In the most basic understanding of the term, "ecological thought" considers the relation of system and environment, perceiver and perceived, as reciprocal: one needs and constitutes the other; one cannot do without the other. However, this does not need to mean that any phenomenon viewed in ecological terms is necessarily one that positively influences all other elements in play. War has its ecology in creating certain perceptual patterns as much as poorly built infrastructures shape how their users perceive and try to make do with them. Moreover, as we know from scientific acoustics, events of resonance do not solely represent the kind of nonhierarchical relationships between nonidentical materialities that cultural critics often see at work when applying ecological thought to matters of culture. Just think of the fact that objects whose vibrations cause other objects to vibrate at the same frequency produce what physicists call "forced vibration." When piano strings trigger the vibrations of a nearby tuning fork and make it sound, the latter resonates with and allows its acoustical potentiality to be activated by the excitations of the former. Although the fork will not become a piano in the process, it is difficult to think of this process as a quasi-nonviolent procedure of reciprocity. Even in the world of physics, then, phenomena of resonance cannot do without one materiality forcing its vibrations onto another. As much as synchronicities can result from two separate objects whose independent frequencies join to form a third, it can also be the effect of one object grafting its vibrations onto another and controlling this second object's ability to swing and swing back on its own terms.

What does this mean for understanding what seems to exceed meaning and understanding in Bay's universe? Sound does many things in his films. We may remember and forget his soundtracks as deafening and restless, but we typically overlook—or overhear—their intricate functions to anchor the visible, set orienting stages for his agitated cinematography, and amplify the pulse of the action. As in conventional filmmaking, sound and music in Bay's work play a key role in stitching narrative elements together, revealing character motivation, and commenting on things that images themselves cannot communicate. In addition, however, sound takes on a crucial function to push the medium of cinema beyond the realms of representation and signification. It features dynamic ecologies of perception and attention in whose context audible vibrations synchronize the rhythms of the action with the rhythms of the viewer. Generous viewers and critics may experience this as an effort to relieve contemporary spectators from the burdens Western culture has placed on the concept of subjectivity. They may cast Bay's sounds as an enactment of sonic materialism, rubbing against the modern construction of the subject as a sovereign, goal-oriented, rational, and primarily visual being. Less generous viewers and critics, on the other hand, may experience Bay's sonic push into the post-representational as a move that is no different from how piano strings force their vibrations onto tuning forks. Bay's sounds, in this understanding, cause viewers to surrender their own sense of rhythm to the excitations of the film they are watching. In doing so, these sounds may replay what Nietzsche and Theodor W. Adorno considered the deeply manipulated operations of Richard Wagner's music dramas: Wagner's effort to engineer the audience's affective responses within his musical structures themselves, his aim to hit his listeners over their heads, and, by folding them into the ecology of his immersive spectacles, to deny autonomous forms of sensory perception.[89]

No matter which position you may choose, it is difficult to deny that Bay's sounds are far from innocent. Though we typically allow his images to make us forget how his soundtracks shape and reshape our attention, Bay's vibrant soundscapes provide instructive models of how to define present and future relationships between different materialities. The audible in Bay's films is a privileged medium to generate effective resonances between mind and matter, animate and inanimate objects, perceiver and perceived, humans and their environments. All of this is just another way of saying that in all of their richness Bay's sounds are deeply political in nature—and most decisively so when we ignore their complex operations as instruments not of attentive listening or signification but of vibrational excitation.

Politics

The opening sequence of Michael Bay's *13 Hours: The Secret Soldiers of Benghazi* intermixes footage from the Arab Spring and the capture of Libya's dictator Muammar Gaddafi in 2011 with images of introductory text flickering on electronic screens, designed to set the tone for a potent story revealing historical truths. Similar to *Pearl Harbor*, *13 Hours* once again relies on Bay's trademark choreography of action and violence to recall factual events. Unlike the earlier film, however, with its ambition to tell an untold story *13 Hours* inserted itself into pressing contemporary political controversies. At the moment of the film's release, disputes about the Barack Obama administration's handling of the Arab Spring and of former secretary of state Hillary Clinton's accountability for the lack of safety of various diplomatic outposts were still raging, spearheaded by various news outlets and members of Congress who were fervently attempting to derail Clinton's anticipated run for the presidential election in fall 2016. The *New York Times*'s Manohla Dargis considered the film politically divisive while admitting that Bay's dramatization of the 2012 attack on the American diplomatic mission in Libya and the murder of Ambassador J. Christopher Stevens would probably not prompt any viewer to reconceive preexisting notions about US involvements abroad: "The movie is unlikely to change the minds of those who subscribe to opposing accounts of the attack, its lead-up, how it went down beginning on Sept. 11, 2012, and the continuing political fallout. Then again, anyone seeking clarity on anything shouldn't look to Mr. Bay; cinematic intelligibility has never been in his wheelhouse."[90] *Forbes* reviewer Mark Hughes, on the other hand, considered *13 Hours* Michael Bay's best movie so far, saying it addressed contemporary issues without taking sides with party politics and felt grittily authentic in spite of various tropes of patriotic fervor and anti-institutional populism. His conclusion: "Don't let politics or ideology or preconceived notions prejudice you against it, it's worth seeing and no matter your party affiliation you will probably find it to be compelling and emotionally engaging."[91] And during a broadcast interview of Bay with Fox News host Bill O'Reilly in January 2016, the latter—to no one's real surprise—praised *13 Hours* for its action-packed realism while the former emphasized his directorial objective to subtract the political from the event's human tragedy and heroism altogether: "We were just saying the facts. Here's the thing: The politics got in the way of this great human story that happened, and this is really to honor these type of men that do this every day—that put themselves in harm's way—that's what this movie is about" (fig. 19).[92]

Figure 19: "Just saying the facts": History according to Bay. *13 Hours* (2016); bottom right: *The O'Reilly Factor* (January 19, 2016, Fox)

TWO WERE IN LIBYA:

THE CIA BASE WAS PROTECTED:
6 ELITE EX-MILITARY OPERATORS.
CODE NAME: G.R.S.

Figure 19: *Continued* |

13 Hours tells the story of six rugged military contractors, stationed in a secret CIA base called the Annex, trying to save American diplomats and personnel on the ground from a vicious attack by local militia on September 11, 2012. Just as Libyan politics after the toppling of Gaddafi appear hopelessly divided between pro-democracy forces and Jihadist fundamentalists, so the American presence in Benghazi and the region in general suffers from a split between idealist political visions of nation building, debilitating political rules of engagement, strategic demands for intelligence gathering, and urgent needs for proficient protection of American lives abroad. After 144 minutes of intense battle scenes, five of the six contractors manage to escort several dozens of traumatized compatriots to Benghazi's airport to await the arrival of another airplane that can transport four dead bodies, including those of Ambassador Stevens and of the contractors' operational leader, back to the United States. Although charged with displays of patriotic sacrifice and resentment of the political establishment, *13 Hours*—perhaps somewhat surprisingly—makes no explicit mention of Clinton's role in navigating diplomatic security concerns. Nor does the film mount a case for any stronger or more militarily decisive American interventions in the Arab world. The film's American mercenaries are tough, defy given chains of command at crucial junctures, and clearly show little respect for political finesse and idealism, but they freely admit to not knowing why Libya really matters to American politics, and they do not hesitate to shed tears about being separated from their families. Benghazi's anti-American militia is presented according to well-familiar anti-Muslim tropes, yet at the end of the film the presence of local pro-democracy forces is required to secure the paths for escape. Some of the film's signals might thus be mixed and square uneasily with how American politicians and media sought to recall the Benghazi event in early 2016 and put such memories to work for domestic political purposes.

Based on the written account of one of the security team's members,[93] Bay's film indeed does everything at its director's disposal to separate telling a tale of military heroism and sacrifice from taking on a clearly identifiable political position. However, Bay's remark that politics got in the way of telling this story properly and that anything political needed to be removed to show the facts and create emotional drama begs more questions than Bay himself sought to answer in his interview with O'Reilly. It makes us wonder what politics for Bay and his films might mean as much as it gives us cause to explore the political import of what Bay, in his intention both to provide captivating entertainment and read history against the grain, considers unpolitical. Any effort to tackle these questions necessarily also raises questions about the politics of the director Bay himself—not in the narrow and rather uninteresting sense of "Is Bay a Republican or a Democrat, a conservative or a liberal?" but in the sense of "What does Bay's alleged depoliticization of the political, his purported privileging of fact over ideology and emotional impact over explicit partisanship, tell us about the political substance of his project of world cinema and cinematic world-making in general? In what way does it comment on the reconfiguration of filmmaking under the aegis of global image proliferation, 24/7 media attention, and populist agendas to make America great again. How, then, can we read Bay's films politically without denying what their maker, and most of their viewers, consider deeply unpolitical about them? What does Bay's claim regarding the nonpolitical nature of his project(s) tell us about the reconfiguration of the political in today's world—a world in which the anti-pluralist and antielitist rhetoric of populist politicians such as Donald J. Trump or Vladimir Putin has become the order of the day?"[94]

Bay's *13 Hours* premiered at the dawn of a year that witnessed a potent rise and return of nationalist populism, rampant anxieties about globalization, anti-institutional outcries of fear and anger, and high-speed social media–based approaches to reshaping public conversations. The world circa 2016 bore little resemblance to how it looked during the post–Cold War era at the beginning of Bay's career, nor even during the post-9/11 period as it hovered ominously above Bay's *Transformers* franchise and its images of Decepticon terror. The election of unlikely presidential candidates such as Donald J. Trump in the United States, the rather counterintuitive vote of Britain to leave the European Union, the upsurge of anti-immigration parties in Western Europe and of anti-foreigner measures in Eastern Europe, the curious blend of autocratic populism and anti-secular nationalism in Turkey, and, last but not least, the lone wolf operations of the Islamic state on Western ground—all indicated the advent of an area when traditional concepts of the political, of political will formation and public deliberation, appeared helplessly out of touch with the realities of epidemic nativism, antipolitical resentment, perceived disenfranchisement, and seemingly random violence on the streets. Although it would be foolish to see Bay's building of cinematic worlds as a direct reflection of or on these diffuse trends, some things that hold for this new era clearly also hold for how Bay's world configures power. For instance, neither Hannah Arendt's notion of power as the capacity of humans to act (nonviolently) in concert for a public-political purpose nor Carl Schmitt's concept of the political as the site at which friends separate themselves in purely formal terms from their foes appears appropriate to describe, let alone understand or critique, what drives politics—the politics of antipolitical and antiglobal resentment, of anti-pluralist and xenophobic contempt—in both Bay's and most of today's world beyond the screen.

More and more often seen as a rigged façade to ongoing states of emergency and the pursuit of personal interest, traditional political institutions and elites today can claim ever less legitimacy to provide what political theorists such as Arendt would have considered the linchpins of power and democratic societies: thoughtful public deliberation and negotiated joint action. In the age of ceaseless Twitter feeds, traditional concepts of publicness appear as muffled as the kind of patience, the ability to listen to the other, it once took to sort out different agendas and construct possible compromises. Sustained attention was critical to what used to count as political debate and decision making. Twenty-first-century media politics, in contrast, increasingly erase what endows political action with robust legitimacy the louder they vie for the public's shrinking windows of attention. On the other hand, in the face of proliferating perceived anxieties about diffuse global threats to given orientations, entitlements, memories, and entire ways of life, little agreement can be found about who might be your friend and who your enemy, even among those who seek to wall in national boundaries. Where Schmitt believed that drawing the line between us and them was the foundational act of the political, today's politics of anger and resentment are constantly haunted by fluctuating assessments of and paranoid responses to external as much as internal challenges. Different structures of antagonism (anti-Islam, anti-Mexican, anti-China, anti-intellectual, anti-gay, anti–you name it) blend into one another without ever producing the kind of homogenous groupings that are essential for what Schmitt considered to be the fountainhead of political action. In this new area of populist obscurity, to rule over the exception is no longer to move the political beyond bourgeois principles of representation, deliberation, and consensus, but to undo whatever we may reasonably call the political to begin with. In the absence of identifiable demarcations between the private and the public, politics has emerged as being everywhere and nowhere while established institutions—such as parliaments, the press, governmental agencies, and constitutional courts—no longer seem to hold the power to mediate between those who are in power and those who are not. Politics is thus reimagined as something in need of neither debate nor anything that may seem to regulate the self-realization of presumable autonomous and atomized social agents.

Understood as a deep, albeit deeply diffuse, mistrust of the political as we have come to know it, the political revolt of the nonpolitical is thoroughly inscribed into the images and narratives of Michael Bay's cinema since the 1990s. It finds its most potent outlet in his uncompromisingly derisive portraits of government representatives, whether they are elected officials, head police or secret service organizations, or communicate a state's needs and visions to foreign populations. Bay's political players are typically shown as driven by selfish agendas, at best incompetent to do their jobs, at worst thoroughly corrupt. They might be Ivy League trained and equipped with superior analytical brain powers, but they normally are in no position to understand the exigencies of the real and the true challenges of actual confrontations. They pretend to know everything about long-term strategy and the big picture but nothing about tactics and goal-oriented action. They live indoors, wear glasses, and look at screens yet instantly falter when it comes to using their fists or putting to work different weapon systems. Their language is refined and their deportment stately as long as any crisis can be held at bay and physical harm does not threaten their own bodies. They wear patriotism on their sleeves while they lack common sense, courage, and savvy. And despite, or precisely because of, their intelligence and instrumental reason, they are easy targets of manipulation, deception, and the stratagems of evil. They never trust anyone, and it would be dangerous to ever place one's trust in them.

There is no need to look far to find Bay's incarnations of tainted leadership and political loftiness as well as the kind of narrative schadenfreude that typically punishes them for their charades, pretensions, dishonesty, and arrogance. Though they often only populate the action's fringes, we find them in almost every one of Bay's features since the early 1990s. Think of FBI Director Womack (John Spencer) in *The Rock*, cooking up elaborate counterterrorism plans yet easily fooled by the cunning of former British spy and long-term prisoner John Patrick Mason (Sean Connery). Think of various police commissioners in the *Bad Boys* sequel, insisting on proper protocol yet precisely thereby threatening successful policing action on the ground. Think of how Washington bureaucrats and the American president (Stanley Anderson) in *Armageddon*, not trusting the ingenuity of Harry Stamper (Bruce Willis) and NASA's ground control in Houston, almost abort Stamper's rescue mission and thereby put the lives of Earth's entire population on the line. Think of the chiefs of staff in *Pearl Harbor*, downplaying possible threats, neglecting analytical data, and ultimately requiring the wit and sacrifice of common soldiers to do their job of protecting the American people. (Jon Voight's FDR here embodies the exception to the rule, his call for resolute action accompanied by images that show him as he lifts himself out of his wheelchair so as to display the need for deeds rather than mere words or thoughts.) Consider various government representatives throughout the entire *Transformers* franchise, without fail getting in the way of much needed interventions, misjudging the perils of Decepticon terror and the benefits of Autobot alliances, and prioritizing personal interest and vanity over common survival.

The representation of the political in *13 Hours* at first clearly follows these formulas. Ambassador Stevens (Matt Letscher) is shown as idealistic, visionary, engaging, and engaged, an advocate of American democratic nation building in the world, a man banking on the presumed rationality and humanity of other political players against all the odds of historical precedent and cultural difference. He comes for a visit to Benghazi partly because he enjoys the city's sense of openness and space; he has little concern for security issues, not least because he envisions the world as if it were a seminar room in which only the best and most persuasive argument may win the day. Although Stevens, unlike many other politicians in Bay's films, has no evil streak about him, it is his political romanticism that not only triggers the siege of the US compound but also costs him and three others their lives. His full name elided, CIA station chief "Bob" (David Costabile) is the recto to Stevens's idealistic, albeit detached verso: a career intelligence officer who is deeply disillusioned and cynical after years of service in the field, evoking proper protocol and hierarchy when tough actions are necessary, hesitating when quick decisions are in demand, eager to protect the purity of long-term strategy and orderly conduct against the messy logic of the real. What Bob may understand as his political work ethic actually serves as a mere shield to protect him from real involvement and hence from protecting those who need protection. He is a loyal servant to the political games Washington wants to play across the world, not to those who face threats on the ground and those who are present to bail them out. His initial reluctance to engage in the conflict is partly responsible for Stevens's death, as much as it leaves him in a complete state of disorientation, of powerlessness and failure. Bob is a figure who is better known to Bay's viewers than Ambassador Stevens: a man in charge, yet void of what it would take to effect things in the world; a leader whose words hide his lack of courage, engagement, care, and responsibility; a bureaucrat whose demand for nonaction creates additional harm and thus serves as both the enemy's fifth column and a narrative negative to which Bay's patriotic mercenaries provide the positive. Bob, and all he stands for, needs to be overcome not only so that lives can be rescued by the hands of resolute men but also so that what audiences typically expect from a Bay feature may kick into action. The politicking of traditional politics needs to reveal its own inadequacy, needs to die, so that what Bay's films present as the nonpolitical resolution of patriotic commitments can show its true life, so that Bay's particular cinema of world-making can live.

None of this should really come as much of a surprise were it not for how Bay's subcontracted and quasi-self-employed members of the security team—the secret soldiers of Benghazi—cast new light onto the director's already familiar contempt for normal politics. As rugged and hands-on as their beards mimic stereotypes of Muslim masculinity, Bay's mercenaries at first recall rank-and-file soldiers of classic Hollywood war films. They may have more muscles, are better at using weapons, and can draw on unparalleled energy levels, but their dedication to their cause, their willingness to sacrifice, and their ability to work around incompetent political leadership recall many models in the history of the Hollywood war genre since the early 1940s. What is strikingly new about Bay's robust warriors, however, is that his six heroes enter, energize, and exit the narrative in the posture of entrepreneurial agents who are deeply affected by how neoliberalism over the last two decades has reshaped economic relationships, social identities, and subjectivities in all branches of life. For them, self-maintenance and self-management counts as the order of the day; they have little trust in nor hope for institutional networks and state-run systems of care; they have learned how to view and market themselves, their expert skills, and their extraordinary combat experience as a form of flexible human capital to be deployed when needed; and they have little patience for regulative processes and hierarchical protocols of interaction. As much as they embody traditional soldierly virtues, their sense of discipline and self-reliance, of working on their own, and of always being "on" without pause and hesitation very much echoes what neoliberal capitalism over the past two decades has come to expect from anyone trying to define himself as a successful economic agent.

Although definitions of neoliberalism vary, most focus on its stress on deregulation, structures of entrepreneurial self-management, and flexible models of work. Under neoliberalism, markets rather than government policies, rugged individualism rather than grown structures of care and solidarity provide the metrics to assess the parameters of a good life. Market rationality, in fact, serves as a model to configure all kinds of social domains and human activities, including those in which money initially seems to play no role whatsoever. Political theorist Wendy Brown therefore suggests viewing the spread of neoliberalism in the new millennium not simply as registering fundamental changes in postindustrial labor practices but as a dynamic by which economic rationality dominates all aspects of life at all times, transforms older models of governance and human identity into forms of management themselves, and replaces the *homo politicus* of ancient philosophy with the figure of the *homo oeconomicus* as the template of social existence: "In neoliberal reason and in domains governed by it, we are only and everywhere *homo oeconomicus*, which itself has a historically specific form. Far from Adam Smith's creature propelled by the natural urge to 'truck, barter, and exchange,' today's *homo oeconomicus* is an intensely constructed and governed bit of human capital tasked with improving and leveraging its competitive positioning and with enhancing its (monetary and nonmonetary) portfolio value across all of its endeavors and venues."[95]

Bay's secret soldiers of Benghazi enter and operate in Libya as both embodiments of neoliberal reason, eager to redefine contemporary warfare as a competitive struggle of flexible human capital, and as subjects who secretly, or not so secretly, suffer from the burdens that the regime of *homo oeconomicus* places on what it means to be human today. Consider the film's principal hero, John Silva (John Krasinski). He arrives in Benghazi as a mercenary with considerable combat experience while his wife struggles at home to raise their kids, maintain their suburban house, and find a way of communicating to her husband that she is pregnant again. His two children implore him not to go or at least to come back soon; his wife has as little understanding of why he needs to offer his skills to conflicts abroad (fig. 20). Like neoliberalism's *homo oeconomicus*, Silva has to be on and flexibly available at all times while conventional boundaries between private intimacy and public activity no longer seem to exist. Economic reason—an ongoing logic of cause and effect, of competitive gain, of navigating a world in which stable social networks and job securities have lost their hold and the labor force has been retrained to self-manage—rules every aspect of his life, including the transatlantic communications that under great time pressure he is able to carry out with his loved ones at home. Success and recognition for his job rests on nothing other than the effective collaboration with his small team, the ability to multitask under duress, his proficiency to adjust strategies on the spot when shifting circumstances require it, and his and his team's confidence to move forward in the absence of traditional hierarchies of command and vetted structures of upward mobility.

Like the self-made entrepreneurs as much as the laid-off workers of our neoliberal age, Silva and his five partners may answer to political imperatives, yet they are shown as having no one really to report to and as operating outside conventional organizational setups. They are literally and figuratively on their own. Silva and his partners initially pride themselves on their atomized status, equating the relative absence of institutional bonds with freedom and liberty. What energizes pride turns into dismay, however, once government commands fail to support the mission of these freelancers—that is, once the very institutions that initially required flexible labor deny their ties and refuse to sign responsible for what they enabled in the first place. Silva's men keep doing their jobs, fighting honorably and bailing incompetent leaders and helpless intelligence agents out of their mess. Yet eventually they no longer do this as proud entrepreneurs but rather in the posture of laid-off workers

Figure 20: Far away from home. *13 Hours* (2016) |

who are compelled to maintain the very logic of self-employment that neoliberalism used to eliminate any kind of common safety net. Secrecy is what energizes these men's sense of importance, but ultimately it also defines the conditions of their disappointment. The secrecy of operating outside traditional structures of work is a primary reason why Silva and his coworkers love their jobs, but it is also shown as something that is damaging to their private relationships, as something that finally causes even manly men to shed tears about the nature of their mission, the isolation in which they operate to safeguard an increasingly elusive sense of commonality.

Though Silva's family is relatively intact, his absence at the domestic front is representative of what we see at work in most of Bay's films: a pervasive trend of displaying the nuclear family in crisis, of showing family constellations that do not match Hollywood's norms of traditional domestic life, and of featuring protagonists that have learned how to make do with what they have. However, what is typically missing in Bay's pictures of the American family, understood as the most basic cell of the social and common, is the figure of the mother rather than the father. In *Armageddon* Stamper raises his daughter, Grace (Liv Tyler), on a drilling rig somewhere in the middle of the ocean as a single parent, with clearly limited pedagogical skills, yet certainly with unrestricted attentiveness. Cade Yeager (Mark Wahlberg), in *Transformers: Age of Extinction*, serves as a single parent of his teenage daughter, Tessa (Nicola Peltz), as a well-meaning but controlling father who, like Stamper, makes do for a mother's absence by trying to shield his daughter with considerable paranoia from any relationship with other men. One protagonist of the *Bad Boys* franchise lives entirely outside of domestic bonds; the other is shown as overwhelmed by familial and marital obligations. The two principal heroes of *The Island*, Lincoln Six Echo (Ewan McGregor) and Jordan Two Delta (Scarlett Johansson), being products of genetic engineering and cloning, know of neither nuclear families nor childhood or teenage existence except through curated images that have been implanted into their memory systems. And while, in the first three installments of the *Transformers* franchise, Sam Witwicky (Shia LaBeouf) emerges from what is probably the most unbroken familial constellation in Bay's films, each of the films leaves little doubt that the at once overbearing and self-centered nature of his parents (Kevin Dunn, Julie White) positions them as relatively unfit to serve the role as parental role models, caregivers, and educative agents.

The nuclear family has long been molded and upheld as both metonymy and synecdoche for the nation-state and the mechanisms of social integration. An ideological product readily exploited by the entertainment industries, the image of the nuclear family has served, and continues to serve, as a grounds to produce ideologies, norms, and values to buttress various visions of the political. In this respect, Bay's repeated figures of broken families, of defunct domestic relationships, of the contemporary American family as a site of absence, lack, and nonnormative engagements might be applauded as a healthy sign of challenging ideological tropes and traditional self-deceptions: a political move that deconstructs normative myths and dispels political fictions that no longer meet the wide diversity of household arrangements, gender constellations, and social practices in the twenty-first century. One might conclude that Bay's films may register that the typical family no longer exists and that in doing so they dismantle its ideological use as a metaphor of the state and the political, urging us to find metaphors elsewhere and to recognize the meaning and viability of what Hollywood in particular often continues to portray as nonnormative social arrangements.

But while it is tempting to read Bay's images of nonconventional family arrangements as potent political interventions, it is difficult to overlook that Bay's assortment of seemingly nonnormative constellations, of single-parent households and often motherless children, is clearly coded as a geography of lack and loss, of diminution in dire need of compensatory activities, as a territory that is still swayed by traditional norms even if Bay's protagonists no longer fully follow all of its trails. The typical family may no longer exist and therefore has ceased to represent or generate the bedrock of state, nation, and politics. However, Bay's heroes still operate under its spell, working twice as hard to ensure that loss does not turn into failure. Whatever breaks Bay's families apart and disperses them into post-traditional diversity, then, also seems to generate the resources that make post-traditional family members want to cope with the end of tradition effectively without questioning tradition itself. Whatever damages the nuclear family energizes its members' hope to start anew, to keep moving and offset the role of missing links.

This ambivalence and ambiguity, I suggest, expresses nothing other than the often Janus-faced logic of neoliberalism itself, the way in which the political push toward deregulation, atomization, and self-management has deeply penetrated the personal and familial. Bay's families are not ciphers of progressive emancipation and diversification but of what neoliberalism has done to the fabric of everyday life over the past two decades or so. They may still operate in the wake of old norms and idols, but in truth they reveal the extent to which even the most basic units of social life today register the political and economic push to treat human existence as an exclusive realm of instrumental rationality, competitive leveraging, and ceaseless self-maintenance. Bay's families, in all of their seeming brokenness and compensatory frenzy, represent what happens when *homo oeconomicus* reigns triumphant and no one can escape being seen and valuated as a flexible form of human capital. Bay's Stampers, Yeagers, and Silvas—like true Heideggerians—may think that moments of danger and disintegration allow saving powers to shine. In truth, however, their response to what they consider as loss relies on and reproduces the very dynamic that caused this loss. To work against what neoliberalist economies did to them, they act as if they wanted to serve as poster children of neoliberalism.

This returns us to the larger question of the political in Bay's films. Like his earlier *Pearl Harbor* and various of his other films, Bay's *13 Hours* is peppered with gestures and symbols of American patriotism, the nation's flag repeatedly appearing as a quasi-sacred icon of collectivity and near-familial belonging that without question justifies sacrifice and pride (fig. 21). While it is easy to dismiss such patriotic postures as mindless jingoism and cheap populism, it is much trickier to identify what makes Bay's project of making America great again often appear so empty of content and proper motivation in his films' narrative contexts, as if it were a sheer automatism, a merely symbolic nod, a memorized invocation that tends to come out of nowhere and has no real anchor in his protagonists' everyday lives. Flags fly, but no one ever details what they may stand for. American lives need to be protected, yet little effort is made to explain whether "American" is to be understood as a cultural, political, constitutional, or ethnic term. US military forces show muscles and advanced weapon systems at work, but they do their jobs best when they are freed from political control or public discourse. Patriotism in Bay's films is something that is seemingly operative without mediation and representation. What may at first serve as a mere symbol—a flag, a military uniform—embodies no less than the nation itself a physical extension of what stirs feelings of belonging and obliges undisputable acts of sacrifice.

Figure 21: Tears for fallen comrades, families, and
nations. *13 Hours* (2016)

And yet in most of Bay's films, including *13 Hours*, patriotism rings
hollow not simply because the nation's body is presented as one gathering
a whole number of phantom limbs but also because the idea of the nation
has become so abstracted from given institutions, constitutional tradi-

tions, and collective practices—from anything political—that it betrays its own status as an empty signifier. Bay's icons of patriotism offer last resorts to all of those who, under the dual pressure of neoliberalism's stress on self-management and the populist rhetoric of antipolitical fear, have lost all access to any viable structure of solidarity and communality, including the traditional family. Patriotism here promises a political sphere cleansed of politics, governments, legal frameworks, open debate, and social obligations—a sphere no different from the classical economic idea of the marketplace in which invisible hands somehow ensure that competitive individualism and instrumental reason do not harm the self-maintenance of others. What appears gung-ho yet ultimately vacant about Bay's icons of patriotism, then, is that his films clearly reveal the extent to which patriotism's promise of collectivity without politics is both a product of *and* a panacea to the neoliberal politics of atomization. Similar to those who embraced Trump in the 2016 election as an authentic voice reclaiming America from foreign powers, Bay's lonely crowds invoke and cling to patriotism as an unmediated structure of belonging because they have come to mistrust any other form of mediation, representation, and negotiated commonality. In this, patriotism serves and is revealed as the opiate of the neoliberal subject. It invites people to promote the demands of deregulated self-management while offering the nation as an answer to the very destruction of sociability and the political neoliberalism has caused. However affective its claim and promise of non-pluralistic unity, the nation in Bay's films—understood as a political space void of politics—does not actually exist. It is a mere specter, a reverse image of the very *homo oeconomicus* that neoliberalism typically celebrates as an antidote to classic concepts of the political, of (big) government, of the social.

This returns us to the point at which we started this book: the question of what it means to speak of "A Michael Bay Film" and of how to situate Bay's project of world cinema and cinematic world-making in the context of filmmaking's past and present. Starring in both *Pearl Harbor* and *Armageddon*, Ben Affleck has not shied away from calling Bay an auteur of first rank: "I think Michael is actually an auteur in the true sense of the word. Every movie he makes reflects his personal creative vision. You may like it, you may not—but those movies are him without compromise. There's something to be said for sticking to your guns."[96]

Affleck no doubt has a point. We certainly know what constitutes "A Michael Bay Film" when we see it. Even films that stand at the margins of his career over the last two decades—the commercial flop *The Island*, the historical epic *Pearl Harbor*, and the contemporary intervention *13 Hours*—are instantly recognizable: their stylistic signatures, formal shapes, narrative energies, and production values tend to stick to one and the same gun. Still, let me suggest in conclusion that what holds for the role of patriotism in Bay's films—a specter that is simultaneously produced by and meant to heal the wounds of the complete reign of market rationality today—may apply as well to our understanding of "A Michael Bay Film" and of what we might want to understand as the politics of authorship in the twenty-first century. As much as it refers to a real person who is zealously involved in many aspects of a film's production, the term "A Michael Bay Film" also functions as a necessary fiction that helps join together the trajectories of diverse labor processes, the work of deregulated human capital, and the subcontracted operations of self-managing entities so as to create a sense of global brand recognition. How is it possible to think of these two, the director and his brand fiction, together?

When French film directors in the late 1950s called for a "*politique des auteurs*,"[97] their ambition was less to hail individual genius or single-handed control over the entire production process than to call for a new form of looking at film and valuing meaningful patterns across a larger body of work. Although auteur theory was often quite critical about the industrial and hence highly collaborative aspects of (studio) filmmaking, it was certainly eager to value authorial signatures in commercially successful films as well, such as those directed by John Ford, Alfred Hitchcock, and Fritz Lang. To speak of authorship was to envision a project rather than to salute existing products; it was to inaugurate a certain way of looking at cinema as if it followed the production modes of other art forms and, in so doing, to discover qualities otherwise left unattended. At its worst, the postwar politics of the auteur resulted in a rather haughty celebration of individual directors as creative virtuosos and a concomitant denigration of the various talents involved in any form of filmmaking. At its best, the concept of authorship encouraged viewers to read films against the grain, to expect more from acts of viewing than simply the repetition of habituated modes of seeing, and to reclaim cinema from all those who simply thought of it as mindless mass culture and "mere" entertainment.

Art cinema today resembles the ambitions of auteur directors circa 1960 as little as the political landscapes of the present recall the structures of enmity during the Cold War, the drive toward globalization after the fall of the Berlin Wall, or even the politics of waging war on terrorism after 9/11. Like cinema in general, art cinema today exists in the plural. It can take place in auditoriums and theaters as much as in gallery spaces, on domestic television screens as much as with the assistance of handheld devices. If film authors once hoped to play out a certain sense of the artisanal against industrial standardization, creative signatures against commercial practices, twenty-first-century media and prosumer culture has leveled traditional boundaries between amateurs and professionals and questioned normative distinctions between art and entertainment, creativity and consumption, activity and passivity. If authorship had once constituted itself as a critical injunction against the streamlined products of the mainstream, the polymorphic nature of commercial filmmaking in the twenty-first century and today's enormous diversity of distribution channels and viewing arrangements situate operative concepts of the past such as "the mainstream," "dominant cinema," and even "Hollywood" as fuzzy and deeply anachronistic, as unable to represent a unified negative to which the art of powerful auteurs could respond as a positive. There is no need to entirely bury the idea of the author and let go of any hope to approach moving-image products as rigorous aesthetic objects. What is certain, however, is that twentieth-century conceptualizations of the cinematic author and their indebtedness to a modernist dialectics of art and mass culture no longer provide what it takes to do justice to the complexities of moving-image culture today.

As foolish as it may seem to call Bay an auteur of action and see his cinema of world-making as a remake of modernist models of artistic creativity and control, the brand called "A Michael Bay Film" offers considerable resources to rethink the politics of authorship in the face of conditions under which cinema has ceased to abide within national borders and domestic film industries. The production, distribution, and consumption of moving images now figures as a highly diverse, often decentered, and yet utterly ubiquitous business; convergence media have long succeeded the former role of the cinematic auditorium as a site to shape our understanding of what it means to interact with motion pictures; and neoliberalism's vision of the *homo oeconomicus* has come to reign utterly triumphant in all arenas of public and private life. Contemporary cinema, argues Jonathan Beller, is characteristic of sociality as a whole: moving images have become so persuasive that cinematic modes of production provide a key to understanding the organization of social relations, labor, sensory perception, and attention in general. In Beller's view, "By some technological sleight of hand, machine-mediated perception now is inextricable from your psychological, economic, visceral, and ideological dispensations. Spectatorship, as the fusion and development of the cultural, industrial, economic, and psychological, quickly gained a handhold on human fate and then became decisive. Now, visuality reigns and social theory needs to become film theory."[98]

Under such conditions, nothing seems more antiquated than to ponder or claim the figure of the auteur, the creative genius seeking to imprint personal signatures onto each and every one of his or her products. And yet, if today even directors such as Michael Bay, as the antithesis of everything art and auteur cinema once seemed to embody, draw on and feed into discourses of cinematic authorship, it would be imprudent to simply dismiss such rhetorical claims as puerile acts of posturing. The most productive question is not "Is Michael Bay an auteur of action, an author of cinematic products as powerful and original as postwar art cinema had once envisioned?" It is "How does what we call 'A Michael Bay Film' today index and reconfigure the very concept of authorship and its politics in twenty-first-century media culture and neoliberal capitalism? And what can social theory learn from 'A Michael Bay Film' in its effort to become film theory?"

To answer these questions, which in essence concern what really matters most about the politics of Michael Bay, we must first once more recall Bay's public image as a resolute director of action films that are widely curated and circulated through celebrity press features, YouTube videos, television interviews, and so forth. Bay is well known to work fast, with incredible energy and zealous effort. He demands tremendous dedication from his production teams and actors, yet he is never shy to take on roles and functions behind the camera that many other directors tend to avoid. He is no intellectual and has little patience for dominant hierarchies of taste. His interviews present him as plain-spoken, with a certain anti-intellectual bent, not daunted by any complexities that may lie ahead of him. Bay embraces the tickle of physical and technological challenges in the production process, his ego apparently in need not to miss any opportunity to applaud his accomplishments. He enjoys controversy and provokes divisive responses to his films or statements, but he also relishes a certain sense of quiet and privacy in his sternly modernist villa in Miami. Actors value his rigorous sense of direction even if at times it may appear exploitative and dictatorial. If you push too hard against Bay's authority, you may lose your assignment. Temporary fallouts, however, may not necessarily result in long-term damages. Bay is a pragmatist, a master of efficiency in all of his excesses; he is not a perfectionist but certainly someone who asks everyone involved in the making of a film to give their best and more. Most of his films cater to some racist sentiments, fly in the face of everyone who wants cinema to abandon its history of sexist images of women, openly serve the agendas of the irrational and immature in his spectators, and engage military personnel and material to appeal to conservative attitudes.

None of this, however, will cause Bay to ever revise his position, rectify presumed misapprehensions, soften stances, build conceptual or emotional bridges, let alone apologize for what may have gone wrong when pressed by his critics. Bay's image is that of the enfant terrible and agent provocateur doing his thing amid a culture industry known for its liberal leanings. He is an autocrat who justifies all means by clearly defined ends and has no trouble admitting that good art, culture, and entertainment do not emerge from democratic decision-making processes and negotiated compromises. If cinema had been around in the early sixteenth century, Machiavelli's *The Prince* may have been one of Bay's counselors. If Bay had been at work during the classical studio era, Erich von Stroheim's jodhpurs, Fritz Lang's monocle, and Alfred Hitchcock's practical jokes—the insignias of directors assuming seemingly god-like powers—would certainly have provided some inspiration for Bay's own self-presentation. Some think of him as the devil, the worst that ever happened to the art of filmmaking, the end of cinema as we have come to know it. But similar to how populist politicians in the age of Twitter turn even negative news into promotional buzz, Bay appears perfectly able to absorb criticism and spin it into marketable publicity—so much so that serious newspaper critics direct little attention to his new releases, and academics have largely decided not to engage with Bay at all despite the fact that global audiences flock in unmatched numbers to the latest Bayhem delivered to their local cinemas.

Nothing we may want to conclude at first could be more contradictory than Bay's public image as muscular and autocratic director and what in the beginning of this book, in response to the sheer magnitude of what we consider "A Michael Bay Film," I called the need to approach his films as hyperobjects, assemblages, and swarms: objects so big that we can no longer think of them exclusively as human affairs; phenomena so complex, flexible, and diverse in gestalt that traditional notions of agency, leadership, centralized control, and directorial oversight simply fail to describe their operations. Social theorists today, when thinking of objects as agential and beyond the grasp of human intentionality, typically do so to envision more sustainable relationships with the world around us and thus level traditional hierarchies between human agents as well. The public staging of Bay as an uncompromising author and audacious creator certainly wants to have none of this, and it is tempting simply to dismiss it as a monstrous return of the past—the Western idea of the sovereign and self-centered individual—in the guise of a narcissist cult of the ego. But to think of his public image as a mere performance that masks or denies the true logic of film production in a global world of flexible human capital and decentered spectatorship certainly misses the point. Instead it is this world's unabashed corollary and dire truth, an outright cautioning not to confuse the reign of *homo oeconomicus* and of complex networks of production with an automatic push toward democratization and liberalization. Bay's performance as an auteur of action is at once a product of and a necessary medium to produce the giant object we call "A Michael Bay Film." It feeds off the extremely differentiated and decentered nature of filmmaking in the present as much as it feeds into it, branding what defies apparent unity and ensuring that one node effectively collaborates with other nodes of production, distribution, and consumption.

In its frenzy to revamp the world as a deregulated market of atomized entrepreneurs, neoliberalism over the last two decades has not only unraveled the fabrics of sociability, the intimate, and the political in all its institutional and constitutional complexity. But in doing so it has also given birth to a new breed of populists, nativists, and demagogues, bridging this very void with promises of strong leadership; with imaginaries of fear, contempt, and patriotic zeal; and with (highly mediated) visions of politics without mediation—politics without normative procedures, regulations, government institutions, and deliberation. Michael Bay's performative image of auteur is to the colossal reality of "A Michael Bay Film" what populist, media-savvy politicians such as Donald J. Trump are to a neoliberal world that they actively helped to deplete of the political in the first place. The performance of Bay as a resolute director who defies elite taste, industry conventions, and discourses of political correctness presents nothing other than the flip side of how cinema has emerged as the dominant mode of neoliberal and globalized production today. One needs another; each sustains the operations of the other. As this book has attempted to show, the films of Michael Bay, amid all of their noise, excess, and agitation, often know more about all of this than their maker is willing or able to admit. Rub somewhat along their spectacular surfaces, and you will recognize the extent to which these films reflect and refract the very dynamic that leads our neoliberal present to embrace quick answers where untidy deliberation might be needed most. Watch them against the grain of their incredible speed, and they divulge what troubles our contemporary moment and cinematic modes of production the most. This is why neither film criticism nor social theory can afford to ignore the hyperobject we call "A Michael Bay Film" and how it redefines what it means to be a human and political being in the twenty-first century.

What has led most scholars to ignore Bay's work in the past also led urban liberals to misjudge the wave that swept populist politicians all the way into the White House in 2017. To better understand Bay's films is to better understand the populisms of our day, no matter whether Bay himself would underwrite them or not: their rhetorical tactics, their appeal to non-pluralistic homogeneity, their desire for simultaneous greatness and boundedness, their paranoid fear of ubiquitous enemies, their contempt for diversity, hospitality, and open-minded care of the vulnerable, strange, or other. If this book succeeds in encouraging viewers (and critics) to take Bay and the politics of his authorship more seriously than in the past, and to recognize that Bay's films like no others represent what cinema is in today's world and might be in the future, it has accomplished its central ambition.

Notes

1. Manohla Dargis, "Review: In Michael Bay's '13 Hours: The Secret Soldiers of Benghazi,' Clarity Isn't the Objective," *New York Times*, January 14, 2016, http://www.nytimes.com/2016/01/15/movies/review-in-michael-bays-13-hours-the-secret-soldiers-of-benghazi-clarity-isnt-the-objective.html.

2. Roger Ebert, review of *Armageddon*, July 1, 1998, http://www.rogerebert.com/reviews/armageddon-1998.

3. Roger Ebert, review of *Pearl Harbor*, May 25, 2001, http://www.rogerebert.com/reviews/pearl-harbor-2001.

4. Peter Travers, review of *Bad Boys II*, July 14, 2003, http://www.rollingstone.com/movies/reviews/bad-boys-ii-20030714#ixzz3zPHvbJhk.

5. David Hochman, "Is Michael Bay the Devil?," *Entertainment Weekly Features*, July 10, 1998.

6. For more about the relationship between filmmaking and natural resources, see Nadia Bozak, *The Cinematic Footprint: Lights, Camera, Natural Resources* (New Brunswick, NJ: Rutgers University Press, 2012).

7. Jean-Luc Nancy, *The Creation of the World; or, Globalization*, trans. François Raffoul and David Pettigrew (Albany: SUNY Press, 2007), 42–43.

8. Dudley Andrews, *Concepts in Film Theory* (Oxford: Oxford University Press, 1984), 38–39.

9. Eric Hayot, *Literary Worlds* (Oxford: Oxford University Press, 2012), 55–60.

10. Henry Jenkins, "Transmedia Storytelling 101," March 22, 2007, http://henryjenkins.org/2007/03/transmedia_storytelling_101.html. See also Henry Jenkins, *Convergence Culture: Where Old and New Media Collide* (New York: New York University Press, 2006), 93–130.

11. Geoffrey Nowell-Smith, ed., *The Oxford History of World Cinema* (Oxford: Oxford University Press, 1999); John Hill, Pamela Church Gibson, et al., eds., *World Cinema: Critical Approaches* (Oxford: Oxford University Press, 2000); Nataša Durovicová and Kathleen E. Newman, eds., *World Cinemas, Transnational Perspectives* (New York: Routledge, 2009); Rosalind Galt and Karl Schoonover, eds., *Global Art Cinema: New Theories and Histories* (Oxford: Oxford University Press, 2010).

12. Siegfried Kracauer, "The Mass Ornament," *The Mass Ornament: Weimar Essays*, trans., ed., and with an introduction by Thomas Y. Levin (Cambridge, MA: Harvard University Press, 1995), 75–88. Kracauer writes about the Tiller Girls: "These products of American distraction factories are no longer individual girls, but indissoluble girl clusters whose movements are demonstrations of mathematics. As they condense into figures in the revues, performances of the same geometric precision are taking place in what is always the same packed stadium, be it in Australia or India, not to mention America. The tiniest village, which they have not yet reached, learns about them through the weekly

newsreels. One need only glance at the screen to learn that the ornaments are composed of thousands of bodies, sexless bodies in bathing suits. The regularity of their patterns is cheered by the masses, themselves arranged by the stands in tier upon ordered tier" (75–76).

13. Francesco Casetti, *The Lumière Galaxy: Seven Key Words for the Cinema to Come* (New York: Columbia University Press, 2015), 213–14.

14. For incisive discussions about the transformations of seeing in the wake of 1960s expanded cinema, see in particular Andrew V. Uroskie, *Between the Black Box and the White Cube: Expanded Cinema and Postwar Art* (Chicago: University of Chicago Press, 2014); Gabriele Pedulla, *In Broad Daylight: Movies and Spectators after Cinema* (London: Verso, 2012); and Kate Mondloch, *Screens: Viewing Media Installation Art* (Minneapolis: University of Minnesota Press, 2010).

15. Jane Bennett, *Vibrant Matter: A Political Ecology of Things* (Durham, NC: Duke University Press, 2009), 24.

16. Sean Fennessey, "Blow-Up: An Oral History of Michael Bay, the Most Explosive Director of All Time," *GQ*, June 27, 2011, http://www.gq.com/story/michael-bay-oral-history.

17. Jussi Parikka, *Insect Media: An Archaeology of Animals and Technology* (Minneapolis: University of Minnesota Press, 2010), xxv.

18. Qtd. in Barry Hertz, "How Michael Bay Transformed the Blockbuster: The Merit behind Michael Bay's Hyper-Aggressive Style of Blockbuster Filmmaking," *McLean's*, June 12, 2014, http://www.macleans.ca/culture/movies/how-michael-bay-transformed-the-blockbuster.

19. Timothy Morton, *Hyperobjects: Philosophy and Ecology after the End of the World* (Minneapolis: University of Minnesota Press, 2013), 1.

20. David Bordwell, "Aesthetics in Action: *Kungfu*, Gunplay, and Cinematic Expressivity," in *At Full Speed: Hong Kong Cinema in a Borderless World*, ed. Esther C. M. Yau (Minneapolis: University of Minnesota Press, 2001), 76.

21. David Bordwell, "Intensified Continuity: Visual Style in Contemporary American Film," *Film Quarterly* 55, no. 3 (2002): 16–28.

22. Matthias Stork, "Chaos Cinema: The Decline and Fall of Action Filmmaking," Indie Wire, August 22, 2011, http://www.indiewire.com/2011/08/video-essay-chaos-cinema-the-decline-and-fall-of-action-filmmaking-132832.

23. Bruce Isaacs, "The Mechanics of Continuity in Michael Bay's *Transformers* Franchise," *Senses of Cinema* 75: Michael Bay Dossier, June 2015, http://sensesofcinema.com/2015/michael-bay-dossier/michael-bay-transformers-continuity.

24. Ibid.

25. Georg Lukács, "Thoughts toward an Aesthetic of the Cinema," trans. Janelle Blankenship, *Polygraph* 13 (2001): 16; originally published in German as "Gedanken zur Aesthetik des 'Kino,'" *Frankfurter Zeitung* 251 (September 10, 1913): 1–2.

26. Rowland Stout, *Action* (London: Routledge, 2005), 3.

27. Interview with Megan Fox, http://www.wonderlandmagazine.com/2009/09/megan-fox-2.

28. Hans Ulrich Gumbrecht, *In Praise of Athletic Beauty* (Cambridge, MA: Belknap Press, 2006), 15–201.

29. Mihaly Csikszentmihalyi, *Flow: The Psychology of Optimal Experience* (1990; New York: Harper Perennial, 2008), 71.

30. G.W.F. Hegel, *Phenomenology of Spirit*, trans. A. V. Miller with analysis of the text and foreword by J. N. Findlay (Oxford: Clarendon Press, 1977), 111–19.

31. "Michael Bay," Urban Dictionary, http://www.urbandictionary.com/define.php?term=michael+bay: "Guy 1: Dude this movie is twitchy and sporadic. It jumps from place to place and nothing is in frame for longer than five seconds. Guy 2: Yeah, that's Michael Bay for you. Don't blame him though, he's got a problem."

32. Malcolm McCullough, *Ambient Commons: Attention in the Age of Embodied Information* (Cambridge: MIT Press, 2013).

33. M. Katherine Hayles, "Hyper and Deep Attention: The Generational Divide in Cognitive Modes," *Profession* 13 (2007): 187.

34. Ibid.

35. Walter Benjamin, "On Some Motifs in Baudelaire," *Selected Writings*, vol. 4, 1938–1940, ed. Howard Eiland and Michael W. Jennings, trans. Edmund Jephcott, 313–55 (Cambridge, MA: Harvard University Press, 2003).

36. McCullough, *Ambient Commons*, 85.

37. Ibid., 86.

38. Jonathan Crary, *24/7: Late Capitalism and the Ends of Sleep* (London: Verso, 2013), 53.

39. F. T. Marinetti, "The Founding and Manifesto of Futurism," in *Futurism: An Anthology*, ed. Christine Poggi and Laura Wittman (New Haven, CT: Yale University Press, 2009), 52.

40. Jim Vejvoda, "Review of *13 Hours: The Secret Soldiers of Benghazi*," January 14, 2016, IGN.com, http://www.ign.com/articles/2016/01/14/13-hours-the-secret-soldiers-of-benghazi-review.

41. Wilhelm Stapel, "Der homo cinematicus," *Deutsches Volkstum* 21 (October 1919): 319, trans. and qtd. in Scott Curtis, *The Shape of Spectatorship: Art, Science, and Early Cinema in Germany* (New York: Columbia University Press, 2015), 204.

42. Tom Gunning, "The Cinema of Attractions: Early Film, its Spectator and the Avant-Garde," in *Early Cinema: Space, Frame, Narrative*, ed. Thomas Elsaesser and Adam Barker, 65–62 (London: BFI Publishing, 1990); and Tom Gunning, "An Aesthetic of Astonishment: Early Film and the (In)credulous Spectator," in *Viewing Positions: Ways of Seeing Film*, ed. Linda Williams, 114–33 (New Brunswick, NJ: Rutgers University Press, 1995).

43. Bruce Bennett, Leon Gurevitch, and Bruce Isaacs, "The Cinema of Michael Bay: Technology, Transformation, and Spectacle in the 'Post-Cinematic' Era,"

Senses of Cinema 75: Michael Bay Dossier, June 2015, http://sensesofcinema .com/2015/michael-bay-dossier/cinema-of-michael-bay-2.

44. Hartmut Rosa, *Social Acceleration: A New Theory of Modernity*, trans. Jonathan Trejo-Mathys (New York: Columbia University Press, 2015).

45. Ira Jaffe, *Slow Movies: Countering the Cinema of Action* (London: Wallflower Press, 2014). See also Matthew Flanagan, "Towards an Aesthetic of Slow in Contemporary Cinema," *16:9: Danmarks klogeste filmtidskrift* 6, no. 29 (2008), http://www.16-9.dk/2008-11/side11_inenglish.htm.

46. Uroskie, *Between the Black Box*, 47–48.

47. Laura Mulvey, *Death 24x a Second: Stillness and the Moving Image* (London: Reaktion Books, 2006).

48. Ibid., 171.

49. Ibid., 176.

50. Ackbar Abbas, *Hong Kong: Culture and the Politics of Disappearance* (Minneapolis: University of Minnesota Press, 1997), 5.

51. Hito Steyerl, *The Wretched of the Screen* (Berlin: Sternberg Press, 2012), 73.

52. Marinetti, "Founding and Manifesto of Futurism," 52–53.

53. Lisa Purse, "Rotational Aesthetics: Michael Bay and Contemporary Cinema's Machine Movement," *Senses of Cinema* 75: Michael Bay Dossier, June 2015, http://sensesofcinema.com/2015/michael-bay-dossier/michael-bay -machine-movement.

54. Lutz Koepnick, *On Slowness: Toward an Aesthetic of the Contemporary* (New York: Columbia University Press, 2014), 25.

55. Eyal Weizman, "Lethal Theory," *Log* 7 (Winter/Spring 2006): 53–77. For more on how Bay's futurist drilling may resonate with the particular exigencies of contemporary warfare and what it does to our understanding of architecture, see Geoff Manaugh, "Nakatomi Space," January 11, 2010, http://www.bldgblog.com/ 2010/01/nakatomi-space.

56. Max Horkheimer and Theodor W. Adorno, *Dialectic of Enlightenment: Philosophical Fragments*, trans. Edmund Jephcott (Stanford, CA: Stanford University Press, 2002), 35–62.

57. J. Bennett, *Vibrant Matter*, 99.

58. Malcolm McCullough, *Ambient Commons: Attention in the Age of Embodied Information* (Cambridge: MIT Press, 2013).

59. Beatriz Colomina, *Privacy and Publicity: Modern Architecture as Mass Media* (Cambridge: MIT Press, 1994).

60. John Durham Peters, *The Marvelous Clouds: Toward a Philosophy of Elemental Media* (Chicago: University of Chicago Press, 2015), 2.

61. Bruce Sterling, "Warchitecture," June 25, 2007, https://www.wired.com/ 2007/06/warchitecture.

62. Peter Zumthor, *Thinking Architecture*, 3rd ed. (Basel: Birkhäuser, 2010), 12.

63. Walter Benjamin, "The Destructive Character," *Selected Writings*, vol. 2: 1927–1934, trans. Rodney Livingstone and others, ed. Michael W. Jennings, Howard Eiland, and Gary Smith (Cambridge, MA: Harvard University Press, 1999), 542.

64. J. M. Bernstein, *Against Voluptuous Bodies: Late Modernism and the Meaning of Painting* (Stanford, CA: Stanford University Press, 2006).

65. Peter Granser and Judith Thurman, "High Aspirations," *New Yorker*, December 14, 2015, http://www.newyorker.com/project/portfolio/high-aspirations.

66. "M House: A Transformer House," August 29, 2013, http://www.busyboo.com/2013/08/29/transformer-house-m.

67. Alexandra Choli, "Bird Island Prefab Homes for Waterfronts in Kuala Lumpur," *Eco Transformer Architecture*, January 29, 2009, http://www.trend hunter.com/trends/sustainability-meets-design-bird-island-project-lands-eco -friendly-hubs-in.

68. Alana M. Klein, *Little Big Men: Bodybuilding Subculture and Gender Construction* (Albany: State University of New York Press, 1993), 41–41; qtd. in Scott Bukatman, *Matters of Gravity: Special Effects and Supermen in the 20th Century* (Durham, NC: Duke University Press, 2003), 61, to whom I am indebted for his insights about the corporeal politics of superhero comics and films in this section.

69. Lisa Purse, "Rotational Aesthetics: Michael Bay and Contemporary Cinema's Machine Movement," *Senses of Cinema* 75: Michael Bay Dossier, June 2015, http://sensesofcinema.com/2015/michael-bay-dossier/michael-bay-machine -movement.

70. Mark Bould, "Transformers," *Science Fiction Film and Television* 1, no. 1 (2008): 166.

71. Lesley Stern, *Dead and Alive: The Body as Cinematic Thing* (Montreal: Caboose, 2012).

72. J. Bennett, *Vibrant Matter*, ix.

73. Prairie Miller, "*Armageddon*: Interview with Michael Bay," no date, http://michaelbay.com/articles/armageddon-interview-with-michael-bay.

74. J. Bennett, *Vibrant Matter*, 12–13.

75. Ian Bogost, *Alien Phenomenology; or, What It's Like to Be a Thing* (Minneapolis: University of Minnesota Press, 2012).

76. Martin Heidegger, "The Question Concerning Technology," *The Question Concerning Technology and Other Essays*, trans. and intro. William Lovitt (New York: Harper, 1977), 28.

77. Ibid.

78. Claudia Gorbman, *Unheard Melodies: Narrative Film Music* (Bloomington: Indiana University Press, 1987).

79. "A Debate with Abbas Kiarostami," *Film International* 3, no. 1 (1995): 47.

80. Lutz Koepnick, *The Dark Mirror: German Cinema between Hitler and Hollywood* (Berkeley: University of California Press, 2002).

81. Steve Reich, "Slow Motion Sound," *Writings on Music (1965–2000)*, ed. Paul Hiller (New York: Oxford University Press, 2004), 26.

82. Michael Coleman, "SoundWorks Collection: The Sound of *Transformers: Dark of the Moon*," https://www.youtube.com/watch?v=E8qX1PoilG4.

83. Isaacs, "Mechanics of Continuity."

84. Bruce Bennett, "The Cinema of Michael Bay: An Aesthetic of Excess," *Senses of Cinema* 75: Michael Bay Dossier, June 2015, http://sensesofcinema.com/2015/michael-bay-dossier/cinema-of-michael-bay.

85. Marc Cotta Vaz, *Visions of Armageddon* (London: Titan Books, 1998), 38; qtd. in B. Bennett, "Cinema of Michael Bay."

86. Jonathan Sterne, *The Audible Past: Cultural Origins of Sound Reproduction* (Durham, NC: Duke University Press, 2003) 15.

87. See, among various other sources, David Abram, *The Spell of the Sensuous: Perception and Language in a More-Than-Human World* (New York: Vintage, 1997); Christopher Cox, "Beyond Representation and Signification: Toward a Sonic Materialism," *Journal of Visual Culture* 10, no. 2 (2011): 145–61, Salome Voegelin, *Sonic Possible Worlds: Hearing the Continuum of Sound* (London: Bloomsbury Academic, 2014); Frances Dyson, *The Tone of Our Times: Sound, Sense, Economy, and Ecology* (Cambridge: MIT Press, 2014).

88. J. Bennett, *Vibrant Matter*, 99.

89. Theodor W. Adorno, *In Search of Wagner*, trans. Rodney Livingstone (London: Verso, 2005); Friedrich Nietzsche, *Friedrich Nietzsche on Wagner: The Case of Wagner, Nietzsche Contra Wagner, Selected Aphorisms*, trans. Anthony M. Ludovici (Edinburgh: T. N. Foulis, 1911).

90. Dargis, "Michael Bay's *13 Hours*."

91. Mark Hughes, "Review: *13 Hours: The Secret Soldiers of Benghazi* Is Michael Bay's Best Film," January 15, 2016, http://www.forbes.com/sites/markhughes/2016/01/15/review-13-hours-the-secret-soldiers-of-benghazi-is-michael-bays-best-film/4/#4487a1fe3e4c.

92. Bill O'Reilly, "Michael Bay Defends Benghazi Film '13 Hours': 'It avoids the politics,'" *No Spin Zone*, January 20, 2016, http://www.foxnews.com/entertainment/2016/01/20/michael-bay-defends-benghazi-film-13-hours-it-avoids-politics.html.

93. Mitchell Zuckoff, *13 Hours: The Inside Account of What Really Happened in Benghazi* (New York: Hachette Book Group, 2014).

94. The following pages are particularly indebted to Jan-Werner Müller's timely and untimely elaboration in Jan-Werner Müller, *What Is Populism?* (Philadelphia: University of Pennsylvania Press, 2016).

95. Wendy Brown, *Undoing the Demos: Neoliberalism's Stealth Revolution* (New York: Zone Books, 2015), 10.

96. Sean Fennessey, "Blow-Up: An Oral History of Michael Bay, the Most Explosive Director of All Time," *GQ*, June 27, 2011, http://www.gq.com/story/michael-bay-oral-history.

97. François Truffaut, "Une certaine tendance du cinema français," *Cahiers du Cinéma* 31 (1954); trans. and reprt. as "A Certain Tendency of the French Cinema," *Movies and Methods*, ed. Bill Nichols (Berkeley: University of California Press, 1974), vol. 1, 224–37.

98. Jonathan Beller, *The Cinematic Mode of Production: Attention Economy and the Society of the Spectacle* (Hanover, NH: Dartmouth College Press, 2006), 2.

The Rebirth of Optimus Prime: Behind the Scenes with Director Michael Bay

By Scott Brown
June 27, 2007

For two glorious years, Optimus Prime was America's hero. He starred in *Transformers*, a thriftily animated series (cynics would call it a half-hour toy commercial) that pitted Prime and his army of Autobots against the vicious Megatron and his Decepticons. On the small screen, these robots in disguise were more than cartoons; they were towering titanium gods, massive in their machine carapaces: tractor trailers, cop cars, fighter jets.[1]

In toy form, Transformers combined the tantalizing tactility of a Rubik's Cube with the vroom-vroom automotive voyeurism of Hot Wheels. Add a touch of Cold War moral clarity and we were hooked. Boys ages 5 to 11—and it *was* boys—faithfully tuned in week after week to watch the saga of these doughty bots, who struck out from their home planet, Cybertron, with vague and mixed motives—conquest, freedom, resources, defense—and brought their civil war to our planet. We welcomed them as liberators and adopted Prime as our mech-daddy. Some quite literally: In 2001, a 30-year-old National Guardsman from Cuyahoga Falls, Ohio, legally changed his name to Optimus Prime. "I really latched onto him when I was a kid," Prime said to TV reporters before shipping out to the Middle East in 2003. "My dad passed away and I didn't really have anybody around."

Then in 1986, the original Prime did something that distinguished him from most other cartoon heroes. He died. He died for freedom, for righteousness, and for shelf space. In the toy biz, there's no room for fatherly affection—only next year's line. *The Transformers: The Movie*, released in August of that year, was Prime's swan song. For nearly two decades, through various toy lines and dubious toon reboots (a gorilla named Optimus Primal? Please.), the sons of Prime waited for Papa Bot.

At last, in July 2004, it was decreed from the throne of Steven Spielberg: There would be a live-action remake of *Transformers*. (Wonder! Joy! Blogging!) A year later, another revelation: Michael Bay, best known for such Truffautian explorations of modern manhood as *Armageddon* and *The Rock*, would direct. (Rage! Spittle! Blogging!)

A prayer went up across the Internet: *Please, God, don't let Michael Bay screw this up*. Debate rocked the virtual halls of nerd Thunderdome, aka Ain't It Cool News, where *Transformers* (out July 4) racked up more traffic than any other upcoming film—no mean feat in the Spidey-infested, franchise-fueled summer of '07. "It was as if you told them Michael Bay was directing *Star Wars*," says Harry Knowles, editor of Ain't It Cool News. "I don't get it, because the things that Bay does best are make cars look cool, make things blow up. He's the best exploder in the business."

So why all the grief over a Bay-battered *Transformers*? It's a toy. A cartoon. What's next? *Please don't let Brett Ratner desecrate the Care Bears*? And aren't ass-kicking robots exactly what you'd expect from the high priest of high-octane puerility?

But among a certain sect of geekdom, there's more at stake. Prime practically step-parented the latchkey kids of the mid-'8os. He was our Allfather at a time when flesh-and-blood role models were increasingly few and far between: Stallone had begun his long sag. Arnold was already more credible as machine than man. So when Prime declared, "One shall stand, one shall fall!" in that seismic, tear-down-this-wall timbre of his (or, more accurately, voice actor Peter Cullen), you believed him. Thus began the cyber-outsourcing of masculine heroism, a process that would eventually, inextricably, link Y chromosome to Xbox.

"I've heard so many people say, 'Michael Bay, you've destroyed my childhood,'" says the man himself from the cathedra of his Santa Monica, California, editing bay. Appropriately, Bay is wearing a black Decepticons T-shirt. He's aware of his image and, to some extent, relishes it. "I knew there were fans," he sighs, shaking his shaggy blond power-mane. "I didn't know there were people who'd hunt you down. I urge them to watch the 1986 animated movie, go watch the cartoon. You'll want to shoot yourself."

True, standards for TV animation have risen—epochally—since the days of those schematic, shakily drawn morality plays, and in theaters, we've been fed ever-more-smashing CG spectacles. But man-children of a certain age look to this Transformers movie—by the director's own admission, a film designed for 9- to 15-year-olds—for more than galvanic summer thrills or simple nostalgia. They're looking for redemption, as men. They're going to a kids' movie to grow up all over again, to re-member just what Prime père taught them before giving up the ghost (and the hallowed Autobot Matrix of Leadership) in '86.

"While a large chunk of people want to see giant-robot fights, there's an equally large, dedicated group who want to see their childhood idols treated like serious characters, with real emotional arcs," says John Rogers, the original screenwriter for the movie. "For every fan wanting to feel like he's 12 again, there's another who's outraged that you think this is just a movie for 12-year-olds. It's not that people don't trust Michael Bay. It's that the list of people who would be trusted is almost vanishingly small."

Trust is in short supply for good reason: We're tired of seeing our childhood titans (Daredevil, Ghost Rider, Catwoman) humbled by heedless, ham-fisted directors. "At best, it will be a fun summer movie with explosions," one 35-year-old Transformers devotee conjectured at a recent WonderCon. "But it seems like guys in Hollywood . . . Unless they're really reined in, they have to pee all over something to make it theirs, like big cats."

The mark of Bay on Hollywood filmmaking is acrid and highly identifiable. He's more jock than geek, a two-for-flinching type who, at 42, is really too old to have any actual Transformers nostalgia of his own. What he does have, though, is a sensibility—a crass and desensitizing one, according to his many critics. *Bad Boys*, *Armageddon*, and the historically hyperbolic *Pearl Harbor*—these movies, with their tommy-gun jump cuts, their nitric, breezily nihilistic momentum, their catchphrase-grunting action heroes, and their napalm denouements, comprise a subgenre known simply as "Michael Bay."

"It's just a style," Bay says, innocent as a killer cyborg lamb. "When Orson Welles loaded all those cinematic tricks into one movie, they hated him for it." (A more historically accurate connection between the two directors might be the fact that one of Welles' last performances was as the voice of Unicron in *The Transformers: The Movie*.)

"Michael Bay" means, among other things, car chases. So, as you might expect from a Michael Bay movie about robots that turn into vehicles, *Transformers* contains a car chase guaranteed to hit fans in their crumple zone. A car chase so smashtacular, he may never do another one.

Watching the scene from Bay's monitors (with Bay helpfully replaying the sequences he doesn't think you've fully appreciated), one can't help but believe him: Down a crowded freeway streaks benevolent Bumblebee, now a yellow Camaro (muscled up from his origins as a VW Beetle). He's carrying our human heroes, teenagers Sam (Shia LaBeouf, breakout star of *Disturbia* and the newly announced *Indiana Jones* sequel) and Mikaela (Megan Fox, in the role of standard Bay hottie), in the backseat. Behind them chugs Prime, in roaring-semi mode, fending off a massive minesweeper called Bonecrusher, an evil Decepticon.

At 90 miles per hour—and here's where the brain begins to record-scratch a bit—Bonecrusher transforms into a bipedal robot the size of a small building. He then rollerblades (there's no other way to describe it) through the traffic, effortlessly sweeping unlucky commuters out of his path. Prime morphs, too, going from hog-nosed Peterbilt to hulking robot in a headlong flinging of struts and panels, digging his big blue clodhoppers into the asphalt and reversing course.

Prime and Bonecrusher collide with molar-rattling impact, then tumble vertiginously over the concrete lip of the overpass to the roadway below, where Prime slams a boxcar-sized fist into Bonecrusher's jaw. Bonecrusher's face erupts in a skittering, dazzling spray of CG shrapnel. Oh, the lack of humanity!

How does this kind of catastrophe happen? With hard work, strict storyboarding, and a computing capacity that is measured not in megs or gigs, but in assloads. In scenes with multiple robots, rendering a single frame of film can take up to 38 hours. "Dealing with the moment where the trade-off from semi wheels to robot feet happens was the most challenging part of the transformation," recalls Industrial Light & Magic's Scott Farrar, who served as visual effects supervisor. "It was important to Michael that they transform in a believable way." (Believability isn't cheap: Production on the movie cost $150 million. Still, that's about half as much as every other blockbuster out this summer.)

Then there's the matter of matter. Bay says that weight-mass orthodoxy informed the decision to make Prime a hog-nosed semi instead of the flat-front model from the cartoon, which, he says, would have yielded only 23 feet of robot height. (He wanted Prime to stand at least 30 feet tall.) He also insists that it was these practicalities—and not his movie's partnership with Chevy—behind his heretical decision to convert cuddly Bumblebee into a bitchin' Camaro. Physics also informed the decision to make Megatron, originally a pistol, into a jet; and Frenzy, the beloved Decepticon cassette tape, is now a shiny boom box. But other alterations were simply Bay's prerogative. Optimus Prime now boasts bright orange cholo flames and—much to fans' horror—lips. "I'm the director. I make my own decisions. I like to paint the house green, even when everyone says it's got to be white."

Bay likes to work fast and acknowledges a tendency to push his crews to the limit. "I've been directing since I was 24. I don't take 'no,' you know? I'm blunt, and sometimes people don't like blunt. But I can run a gigantic ship, on 12-hour days, without going into overtime."

Bay can probably afford to pay overtime. Thanks to the success of *Pearl Harbor,* Bay has built up so much goodwill with the Pentagon that he can call up and order F 16s the way the rest of us order hot wings. What's more, this movie's theme—"No sacrifice, no victory"—certainly must resonate with the military mindset right about now. An excellent way to keep costs down is to get aircraft, tanks, technical advice, locations (Edwards Air Force Base, White Sands Missle [*sic*] Range), and already-costumed troop extras on the cheap.

"When Hollywood comes to us for assistance, we see it as an opportunity to inform the public about the US military," says Phil Strub, the Pentagon's Hollywood liaison. "If they want our help, they have to show us the script and listen to our suggestions for increasing the military realism." Bay puts it a little more bluntly: "I think they look at it as a recruitment thing."

In the movie, the Decepticons make their first attack in the Middle East, and the war comes swiftly home to Anytown, USA. What does the Pentagon, or Bay, for that matter, think of a story that puts the American military in the middle of an alien civil war? Bay brushes off any parallels. "Civil war? Well." He pauses. "A good movie teases you!" He pauses again. "There's a lot of good action here."

A lot of good product placement, too. In addition to Detroit's most-steroidal rides, you'll see a transformational cell phone and videogame console. Bay notes that he "took it up the ass" for product placement on his last movie, the box-office bomb *The Island*. (In its bold vision of the future, Aquafina, Michelob, and Cadillac featured big—though it should be noted that Spielberg, Bay's *Transformers* producer-collaborator, pulled the same trick with *Minority Report* and got little guff for it.) But let's be honest with ourselves, purists: Are we really going to quibble about endorsements when the urtext itself was fired in the kid-vid kiln of product placement? "What do you want, speeches at the UN?" co-screenwriter Roberto Orci asks. "It's *Transformers*."

True. But pimping our childhood ride is one thing; pimping our dad is another. With bated breath and shaken faith we await the return of our Almighty Rig. Because without Prime, we're stuck with whiney Spider-Boys, metrosexual pirates, and koan-spouting kung-fu Christs in designer sunglasses and unisex clubwear. Because he died protecting us in '86, and nothing's ever been the same since. Because these days, the only real men left are giant robots. It's moot, of course: With or without the sons of Prime, *Transformers* will do zero-to-bank in four seconds. Still, we wonder: When Papa comes truckin' home, will we recognize him?

Blow-Up: An Oral History of Michael Bay, the Most Explosive Director of All Time

By Sean Fennessey

June 27, 2011

Actors have called Michael Bay an asshole, a cocksucker, a Nazi—often to his face—and then swiftly signed up for the sequel. As America braces for the third chapter of Transformers—the latest explode-a-thon from the director of *Bad Boys*, *The Rock*, and *Armageddon*—dozens of his collaborators and victims, from Will Smith to Steven Spielberg to Scarlett Johansson, reveal the secret genius behind a true Hollywood visionary. (And yes, we're still talking about Michael Bay.)[2]

"Loud." "Stupid." "Horrible." "Unbearable." "Appalling." "Evil." "A great grinding garbage disposal of a movie." "An assault on the eyes, the ears, the brain, common sense and the human desire to be entertained."

In 1998, a national magazine asked in an article "Is Michael Bay the Devil?" Thirteen years later, you can still buy T-shirts that answer yes. The 46-year-old director has long been treated by cineastes as the macho spawn of Ed Wood—a testosterone-sweating embodiment of everything that is wrong with modern Hollywood. (Those quotes up there are from actual reviews of his movies.) It also doesn't help his image that on his film sets he can be a notoriously domineering prick. Bay has flourished, though, not just because his eye-strafing event movies rake in so much money but also because—and let's whisper here, lest the film snobs are listening—*so many of them kick ass*. Sure, the dialogue is often subliterate and his fast-cutting style can cause epilepsy. But! Movie stars look dripping hot, never better, in front of his camera. And of course, he has orchestrated some of the most complex and thrilling action set pieces ever put on film. Is Michael Bay an artist? Uh, no. But is he a movie icon? Have you *seen* the car chase in *Bad Boys II*? As opening day approaches for *Transformers: Dark of the Moon*, more than sixty of Bay's friends, relatives, actors, and collaborators testified to *GQ* about the most underappreciated man in show business.

GABRIELLE UNION (ACTOR, *BAD BOYS II*): You know when people talk about the very first time they did drugs? Being in a Michael Bay movie was like my drug. It's like I'm chasing the dragon—I've been chasing that experience ever since.

JAMES CAMERON (DIRECTOR): I've studied his films and "reverse-engineered" his shooting style. He loves what I call "the big train set," huge physical production, just as I do. It is the most challenging type of filmmaking, and he does it gorgeously.

BEN AFFLECK (ACTOR, *ARMAGEDDON, PEARL HARBOR*): I think Michael is actually an auteur in the true sense of the word. Every movie he makes reflects his personal creative vision. You may like it, you may not—but those movies are him without compromise. There's something to be said for sticking to your guns.

STEVEN SPIELBERG (PRODUCER, *TRANSFORMERS*): He has the best eye for multiple levels of pure visual adrenaline.

FRANCES MCDORMAND (ACTOR, *TRANSFORMERS: DARK OF THE MOON*): Michael Bay has a mainline to the testosterone glands of the American male.

JOHN TURTURRO (ACTOR, *TRANSFORMERS*): He likes blowing things up.

ROBERTO ORCI (SCREENWRITER, *TRANSFORMERS*): We're aware of how some people think, in terms of film history, he's the Devil. But it's amazing to have a movie where you can look at five minutes and go, "That's a Michael Bay movie." To have a style that distinct—like it or hate it, it deserves study.

GEORGE LUCAS (DIRECTOR): Michael's films are immediately identifiable.

EHREN KRUGER (SCREENWRITER, *TRANSFORMERS: Dark of the Moon*): He's like this cross between General Patton and Willy Wonka. He's in command of a massive army, all in the effort to create the ultimate Everlasting Gobstopper.

JEANINE BASINGER (BAY'S FILM PROFESSOR, WESLEYAN UNIVERSITY): I always tell my husband, "My tombstone is going to say, 'She taught Michael Bay.'"

MICHAEL BAY: I'm, like, a true American.

In Which We Glimpse Our Hero in His Youth

Michael Benjamin Bay grew up in a middle-class household in Southern California, the adopted son of Jim and Harriet Bay. In school, he had trouble focusing—what would probably now be diagnosed as ADD—but showed an early talent for physics, photography, the making of things.

BAY: I grew up in the Valley. My dad was an accountant, my mom was a therapist for kids.

BRAD FULLER (PARTNER, PLATINUM DUNES, BAY'S FILM COMPANY): I met him at Hebrew school, but I think he denies that.

BAY: I was a shy kid, but I was very good at baseball for my age. I won MVP many times. I was like a quiet jock. I also did theater. I did *The Pirates of Penzance*. I had to memorize an hour and a half operetta.

HARRIET BAY (MOTHER): He was the lead, singing Frederic. I never laughed so hard in my life.

BAY: I was into these very advanced trains [*sic*] sets, with towns and cities and whatever, the detail of it. I remember my parents came to me: "Michael, we think you need to get outside more." And I'm thinking, "Am I fucked up?"

HARRIET BAY: Some people these days call energy like that ADD-kind of energy.

K. C. HODENFIELD (FIRST ASSISTANT DIRECTOR, VARIOUS BAY FILMS): I had started a softball team at Lucasfilm, and there was this whiny teenage kid who would come around with the president of the company's son, wanting to play in the games. So I gotta get this kid some playing time. Ends up it was Michael Bay.

IAN BRYCE (PRODUCER, VARIOUS BAY FILMS): In 1980 I was parking cars at Lucasfilm, and Michael was a summer intern; he was filing *Raiders of the Lost Ark* storyboards in the photo department.

BAY: I was 15. The first thing I ever said to Steven [Spielberg] was, "I really thought *Raiders of the Lost Ark* was going to suck."

After high school, Bay moved across the country for an unlikely destination: Wesleyan University, a tiny liberal-arts school in rural Connecticut known for its antimainstream intellectualism. He did not fit in.

FULLER: I wonder if he'll admit this: we both did poorly on our SATs.

HARRIET BAY: He probably has the lowest SATs of anyone who ever went to Wesleyan. But he's just not a good test-taker. He graduated magna cum laude.

BAY: Wesleyan was very cliquey. They all wore dark clothing, and they were always uggghhhhh.

BASINGER: "All the film majors wore black! They liked death!" He sees them as one giant goth! Wesleyan was not a very big frat school, but Michael belonged to one.

FULLER: We were very outspoken that there's nothing bad about making commercial films, and we were certainly ostracized by some of our classmates for that. We both loved *Risky Business.*

BASINGER: *West Side Story*—that film in particular captured his attention.

BAY: I thought, "Musicals? Ugh, what am I doing? I don't want to take a musical class. Sounds terrible." I loved it. It was all about form, style, how they use the medium. That's what I try to do with my action.

BASINGER: That class was important to him, because he realized that you're not bound by reality in film if you don't want to be. And his work is about color and movement and a kind of abstraction and unreality that is found in musicals.

In Which Our Hero Narrowly Avoids "Movie Jail"

In the early 1990s, Bay quickly became a coveted music video and commercial director, amassing a body of work known as much for its sharp humor as for its bold pyrotechnics. Among his work: the original Got Milk? advertisement and an epic trio of music videos for Meat Loaf.

BAY: I knew exactly what I was going to do. I was going to do videos—that's when videos were fun. And then commercials—I was told, "Oh, you can only do one type of commercial. You can do sports. Or action. Or comedy." But I'm like, "I'm gonna do 'em all."

TONY SCOTT (DIRECTOR, *TOP GUN, DAYS OF THUNDER*): Michael and I come from commercials, we come from videos. And what that means is, we're practiced in shooting on tops of mountains, underwater, with actors and non-actors, with models—we've created our craft, because we get to try things all the time.

BAY: This guy called me in from Capitol Records—he was a hard-ass marine, kinda scary in the meeting. He said, "If you can wrap this Donny Osmond video up for $165,000 . . ." Meanwhile, I'm like two weeks out of school. The most I've ever spent is $5,000. I ended up getting paid $500. But I got to make my first thing.

HARRIET BAY: I remember going out to watch him shoot it. It was in the Mojave desert, and there's like 200 people. It's this big deal. It was so exotic. It was the first time he got to use a helicopter. And he whispers in my ear, "Mom, can you believe I'm getting paid to do this?"

FULLER: The first time I saw Michael on a bigger set, he was doing a video, and there was the hottest blonde girl I've ever seen in my life, and she's got a wind machine on her. She's dancing, she looks hot, she's wearing a short skirt. He's shooting her from a low angle. And he looked at a few of us, and there was this look in his eyes, like he had reached nirvana. It was childlike wonderment.

BAY: Soon I got called by Propaganda Films. It was just a creative little hub making videos and commercials. It was David Fincher, Dominic Sena, Nigel Dick, Greg Gold. Fincher—at one point our offices were across from each other, and I always called his The Doom and Gloom Office because it was always dark. And I was "The commercial guy."

ROBBIE CONSING (STORYBOARD ARTIST, VARIOUS BAY FILMS): I remember a lot of my director friends and bosses at the time were wary of Michael, this kid rising up so quickly, still in his early twenties. And those wary directors were only in their late twenties and early thirties themselves.

BAY: The offer to do Got Milk? came to me and I'm like, "Milk? That's embarrassing." When I did it, I was like, "This is a terrible commercial. I don't get it." It won the Grand Prix Clio for Commercial of the Year. I think it's an OK commercial.

SCOTT GARDENHOUR (PRODUCER): There was no question Michael would go on to do other things, and that they wouldn't be small.

BAY: I had gotten movie offers and turned them down. I took my time. They sent me *Saving Private Ryan*, but I wouldn't have known what to do with it.

JOE PANTOLIANO (ACTOR, *BAD BOYS*): I remember Don Simpson and Jerry Bruckheimer had this movie *Bad Boys* going. It was going to be Jon Lovitz and somebody else—

JERRY BRUCKHEIMER (PRODUCER, VARIOUS BAY FILMS): Dana Carvey. We'd looked at a bunch of commercial directors because we'd had success with Tony Scott, and the one reel that stood out was Michael's. It had a wonderful sense of humor and a unique visual style—like nobody else. Michael did a test scene with Jon and Dana, but Disney didn't like the test.

BAY: Jeffrey Katzenberg didn't think it was funny. Maybe it was too goofy.

BRUCKHEIMER: So we took the movie to Sony, and they wanted Arsenio Hall, because he was a big star at the time. I didn't think that was going to work. So then they said, "What about Martin Lawrence?"

MARTIN LAWRENCE (ACTOR, *BAD BOYS*): There were a few names [for the other lead]. Like Laurence Fishburne. I was riding down the street one time and I saw him, so I yelled out of the car, asking if he would do *Bad Boys*. Laurence Fishburne shook his head no. And then Michael kind of handpicked Will [Smith].

BRUCKHEIMER: I think Arsenio turned it down, is what really happened. So we convinced them to use Will.

WILL SMITH (ACTOR, *BAD BOYS*): My first impression of Michael was that he was like . . . you know how at the go-kart races, there's always one kid who's got real wheels on his go-kart and everybody else got the plastic baby wheels? That one kid who always had it elevated? That was Michael. I think he had just done the Meat Loaf video—this guy had a *plane crash* in a *music video*. I was like, *Damn*.

JENNIFER KLEIN (PRODUCER; FORMER VICE PRESIDENT, BAY FILMS): There was no script when they started filming *Bad Boys*.

FORM: Well, there was a draft, but yes, there were new pages being slid under doors at night in the hotel.

BAY: I was fearful of movie jail. Movie jail is: you screw up your first time, you're never working again.

BRUCKHEIMER: He pushed really hard—the first day of filming, he did like fortysome setups. A normal director—you get ten, if you're lucky.

SMITH: The set, it was probably dangerous.

BAY: By week two, Martin was being a dick to me. And I was like, "What is this attitude?" He didn't trust the white man. That was the deal.

LAWRENCE: That's exactly what it was. You know, Michael—he has a certain bravado. One time he said to me, "I need your notes on the script," and I looked at him, I said: "Michael, yeah, I'll get the notes to you when I get to it." And he just looked at me with this blank stare like, "Oh, he did *not*."

BAY: [Eventually] I took him aside and said, "Dude, what's your deal? I'm busting my ass to make you look good, make you look funny. And you just keep belittling me." And then here's the speech, almost like it was ready to come out. He says, "I'm a black man that made it from nothing!" And I said, "You know what? I'm a white guy who made it from nothing, too. I grew up in the fuckin' Valley." Instant respect.

LAWRENCE: I had to get to know him. We grew to be the coolest.

PANTOLIANO: Michael would say, "Look, I only got $23 million, okay?

FORM: It was only a $19 million movie. Which no one believes, but it's true. I have the budget.

BAY: Maybe I had $11 million.

BRUCKHEIMER: Michael even had to write a check for an action sequence that Sony wouldn't pay for.

BAY: The scene where Martin shoots the guy out of the plane. I said to the line producer, "This is where the audience claps. This is the end of the movie." He was like, "I don't care. We're not doing the shot." He was just a studio flunky. I was literally going to punch him out.

PETER DEVLIN (SOUND MIR, VARIOUS BAY FILMS): The scene cost $25,000. That's a lot of money. I believe the studio cashed the check as well.

BAY: They used to watch dailies where you do the *clap* with the slate. So just to screw with them, I put the check [on the slate and wrote] TO COLUMBIA PICTURES, FROM MICHAEL BAY, $25,000.

BRUCKHEIMER: He put his money where his talent is.

BAY: I didn't get the money back until the movie made like $60 million. And I had to beg for it.

KLEIN: There's this scene where Will Smith runs down a street, and at the first test screening in Lakewood, California, women were screaming because Smith's shirt is flying open. That was it. He was a star.

BAY: We had an argument about that shot.

SMITH: He was like, "Oh, take your shirt off and run with the gun!" And I was like, "Come on, man. That's just on the edge of corny." But he can take things that you'd think of as corny, and make it supergalactic iconic.

BAY: I was like, "Look at this! You look like a movie star!" And he's like, "Shit, I do!"

SMITH: That was the moment for me where I learned how important single images are. That single image took me from a comedic television actor to a potential movie star. The scripts that I started to get offered changed dramatically. It was the first time that I heard women react to me with an audible gasp. There was a transformation from the cute guy next door who could make you laugh to a guy who might be able to handle himself in a bar fight and a bedroom.

KLEIN: I don't know that anyone is a starmaker, but I think Michael has a knack for taking actors and actresses and elevating them to another level that they might not have known was within them. Will Smith, Ben Affleck, Nic Cage—like, before *The Rock*, what was he doing?

BAY: I didn't make him a star. Remember, he got the Oscar for Best Actor [for *Leaving Las Vegas*] when we were doing *The Rock*. Which wasn't a no-brainer. We had to do a lot of work on the script to make it more real and serious and cool.

BRUCKHEIMER: On *The Rock*, we had Aaron Sorkin sending us pages almost every day because some of the scenes weren't working.

BAY: I was terrified of working with Sean Connery. I gave him my first great direction: I said, "Can you act less charming?"

BRUCKHEIMER: He did a terrific job of getting Sean to loosen up. I shouldn't say loosen up, because he's pretty loose—getting Sean to accept some of Nic's craziness. I shouldn't say craziness—I should say his creative dialogue.

BAY: One day I showed up on set and Cage came out for a scene in his apartment dressed in a purple Speedo. And I'm like, "Oh, I get it. Okay. You don't want to wear the wardrobe because you want to show your muscles. OK, let's just get it all out in the beginning of the movie."

BRUCKHEIMER: It wasn't always a cakewalk. Sean Connery's like another producer. He'll come out on set and say, "Why is that here? That crane's been out here for two days and nobody's using it. You're wasting money."

BAY: He kept calling me "boy." And one time he called me a "cock." [In Connery accent] "You cocksucker!" It was his last day of the shoot, and he didn't like holding his breath underwater. I had United States SEALs holding him down because there was a fireball going over the water, and if he came up, he would burn his face off. So whatever, he called me names.

In Which *Armageddon* Is Coming (to a Theater Near You)

Bay followed up Bad Boys *and* The Rock *with* Armageddon, *about a giant asteroid on a collision course with Earth. Made for $140 million,*

*the movie grossed more than half a billion dollars worldwide, and it
cemented Bay's reputation as a popcorn superstar and critical Antichrist.*

BAY: I took a geology course with this tectonic expert at Wesleyan.
He said, "Calamities happen; it's the plumbers who will fix the world."
So *Armageddon*—that's what it is, it's everyday Joes saving the world.

MATT COHAN (VICE PRESIDENT, BAY FILMS): I've heard him describe
Armageddon—at least structurally—as a comedy, in the tradition of
the old Laurel and Hardy or Abbott and Costello fish-out-of-water
comedies.

BAY: It's supposed to be a joke. It's about making fun of the system.

OREN AVIV (CHIEF MARKETING OFFICER, 20TH CENTURY FOX): How do
you make the fact that the world is about to blow up seem like a lot fun?

BRUCKHEIMER: We really tried to ground it in some form of reality—even though it's a fantasy. So we did a lot of research and asked
scientists to work with our writers to get as much reality into the movie
as possible.

BAY: The real story is, it's going to happen. Yes, we are going to have
an asteroid hit us again, and yes, the earth will die. Absolutely, 100
percent positive.

BILLY BOB THORNTON: You know, what sets *Armageddon* apart from a
lot of those big splashy movies is, it's actually pretty good. I mean, people
love that movie; it's become kind of an American favorite. One of my
lines is—I don't know if you'd call it iconic, but it's when I'm talking to
the president and he says, "How big are we talking here?" And I say,
"It's the size of Texas, Mr. President."

MATT COHAN: *Armageddon* was pretty notorious for having I don't
know how many uncredited writers working on it, one of whom happened to be Robert Towne.

ROGER EBERT, FILM REVIEW, JULY 1, 1998: "*Armageddon* reportedly
used the services of nine writers. Why did it need any? The dialogue is
either shouted one-liners or romantic drivel. 'It's gonna blow!' is used
so many times, I wonder if every single writer used it once, and then
sat back from his word processor with a contented smile on his face,
another day's work done."

BRUCKHEIMER: Owen Wilson definitely was Michael's idea. Michael
saw *Bottle Rocket*; he said, "We gotta hire this guy."

BAY: [The first day] Owen came to the set an hour, hour and a half late. We put the PAs out on the Warner Bros. lot, said "Call me when you find him." On *Armageddon*, each day was a big expensive day, $250,000. I put my arm around Owen, who's a great guy. I said, "Owen, you know what, I worked with Sean Connery and I gotta tell you, he was never late." And Owen was never late again.

KLEIN: Ben [Affleck] was new on the scene. We put him through the Bruckheimer-Bay machine—like, You're no longer chasing Amy. You're going to have to go to the gym, get a tan, get a haircut.

BAY: Jerry had a problem with his teeth. "He's got baby teeth. I fid [*sic*] Cruise's teeth. We're going to fix his teeth." So Ben got a beautiful set of teeth out of it.

KLEIN: I remember the first day of shooting in Kadoka, South Dakota, and [Ben] was wearing this spacesuit, and he was pissed. You couldn't go to the bathroom in it, it weighed however many pounds, you're sweating, so who are you mad at? Michael.

AFFLECK: I imagined [Michael] would be emblematic of everything big and Hollywood. I had come off *Chasing Amy* and *Good Will Hunting*, so I really had no idea what big Hollywood movies were like.

THORNTON: I was sitting at the table read-through with Owen [Wilson] and Buscemi, and we were all sitting there kind of nervously. And Steve looks at me and goes, "What the fuck are we doing here?"

In Which Our Hero Discovers War Is Hell

By 2001, after three straight monster hits, Bay was the most coveted director in Hollywood. Now the hot-young-filmmaker script called for a bid for seriousness, an attempt to make an "Oscar movie." Pearl Harbor actually did end up winning one—for sound editing. It was also among the decade's worst-reviewed movies.

DICK COOK (FORMER CHAIRMAN, DISNEY): I think *Pearl Harbor* was one of the most difficult shoots of modern history.

CONSING: One day, I was on the way to meeting with Michael on a battleship at Ford Island. Complete Bayhem. I passed a squadron of Zeros chasing two P-40 fighter planes forty feet above the deck, guns blazing, followed by the camera ship. Then watched fireballs exploding on a nearby frigate as burning stuntmen leaped into the water. Then saw another Zero come around and buzz our battleship as Cuba Gooding Jr. fired back with a .50 caliber fifteen feet over my head. It wasn't even 10 a.m.

BARRY WALDMAN (PRODUCER, VARIOUS BAY FILMS): I think the studio tried to shut down the movie twice.

COOK: Michael was putting in twenty-hour days. And he was driving the crew and the performers and everybody crazy.

WALDMAN: We must have blown something up every day.

HODENFIELD: We blew up hundreds of bombs, multiple ships out in the harbor. I had to shut down two interstates. I was like, *Oh, my God—people are gonna think the Japanese are attacking again,* 'cause we were gonna blow this place sky high.

MIKE CASE (VICE PRESIDENT, BAY FILMS): I remember being on that set and listening to his voice as a commander. All hell's about to get unleashed; these bombs are going to go off and these guys need cues. And right then and there, you saw him, almost like he was in battle.

BAY: It was dangerous. A plane hit a palm tree, the thing crashed, and the guy survived—miraculously survived.

AFFLECK: The script was good. The idea was to make the kind of movie that could have been released in the '40s—unironic, slightly naive—with new technology.

KENNY BATES (STUNT COORDINATOR, VARIOUS BAY FILMS): Michael Bay is not gonna tell a love story. It's not because he doesn't care; it's because that's not part of who he is. He's not a terribly sensitive guy. But he's a great filmmaker.

HODENFIELD: Michael was saying he was gonna go about the movie differently—he was gonna hold shots longer, he wasn't gonna move the camera as much. This was gonna be like a classic movie. The first day we started shooting, he wasn't using his fast-moving, fast cuts, low shots—his bag of tricks—and it was like watching an Italian speak without his hands. By lunchtime, we're making a Michael Bay movie, in the Michael Bay style.

BAY: I don't change my style for anybody. Pussies do that.

ROGER EBERT (FILM REVIEW, MAY 25, 2001): "The film has been directed without grace, vision, or originality, and although you may walk out quoting lines of dialogue, it will not be because you admire them."

BAY: It got pounded by critics. It's funny with them. You are making entertainment. People get so angry about it.

BASINGER: I think this kind of thing hurts Michael a lot. He says it doesn't. But I think the ferocity of the animosity aimed at him has shocked him and hurt him.

BRUCKHEIMER: You'd like to get good reviews, but the only reason I still have an office and a parking space at Disney is our movies do well.

HODENFIELD: Honestly, I felt like that movie took some years off my life.

BAY: It was successful. It had a huge opening day, then it started dropping off. But it made $450 million. They said it was not a hit. It was a hit. And then the DVD came out after 9/11 and it became a massive, massive DVD—the largest of all-time, at that time. Because all of a sudden it was cool to be patriotic again.

SHIA LABEOUF (ACTOR, *TRANSFORMER* SERIES): It's the casting. With a different cast, *Pearl Harbor* would be considered a masterpiece.

In Which Our Hero Transforms

The Island, a sci-fi movie starring Scarlett Johansson and Ewan McGregor, became the only true commercial flop of Bay's career. The 2005 film cost $126 million and made just $36 million in the U.S. For the first time, he needed a hit.

ADAM GOODMAN (PRESIDENT, PARAMOUNT): Transformers are essentially cars that change into robots, and who better at shooting cars than Michael Bay?

SPIELBERG: I couldn't think of a better director to turn a truck into a robot and make us believe it was really happening.

BRIAN GOLDNER (CEO, HASBRO): He knew that Transformers existed; he knew that they were robots and cars, but he didn't know all the mythology.

BRYCE: I think Michael would be the first to say that he didn't get it in the beginning.

BAY: I thought it was a dumb idea.

JOSH DUHAMEL (ACTOR, *TRANSFORMERS*): Michael poked his head [into a meeting] to say hello and started telling me about his next project, a movie called *Transformers*. And I go "Transformers? Like the cartoon from the '80s?" and he's like "Yeah, yeah," and he's all excited about it. And I was thinking, *This is the worst idea ever.*

ALEX KURTZMAN (SCREENWRITER, *TRANSFORMERS* SERIES): It's about a boy who's really obsessed with getting a car. That's when we saw Michael's eyes light up like he was a 12-year-old again.

SPIELBERG: It was Michael's sense of humor that would allow audiences to take *Transformers* just seriously enough.

GOODMAN: It became Michael's mission to make the most pop, commercially successful movie he could, because he wanted to. And because he needed to.

BAY: Steven wanted me to do it. It was, like, a kiddie script. He goes, "Michael, I wanna be your new Jerry. How do I compare to him?" So funny. He's like a kid.

LABEOUF: When I met Mike, I was a seventeen-year-old boy. He was my fucking god.

JOHN FRAZIER (SPECIAL-EFFECTS SUPERVISOR, VARIOUS BAY FILMS): I went up to Shia one day and I said, "You just made history. You were involved in the biggest explosion for a motion picture with an actor. You were in it. Usually, you have stunt people in there." Five thousand gallons of gasoline. Probably one hundred sticks of dynamite. You only see that stuff in Michael Bay movies. Nobody else does that stuff.

KURTZMAN: [*Transformers: Revenge of the Fallen*] was a very different experience for all of us, because we agreed to do the movie about two weeks before the writer's strike. So we had those two weeks to outline the story, and then the strike happened and we couldn't continue.

LABEOUF: Everybody felt like, "Well, if there's anybody to do this again, it's the guys who wrote the first one, because the first one's fantastic." We were forced on this fucking script because we had a release date.

ORCI: I remember there was a huge pressure—and not just from the studios—to make our date, but also from Michael himself.

KRUGER: He wasn't thinking so highly of writers at that moment.

ORCI: When we got back from the strike, he locked us in a golden jail. He locked us in the Del Mar Hotel on the beach six blocks from his office so that he could have surprise inspections at any moment.

KURTZMAN: It was simultaneously pressure-filled and amusing, you know?

BRYCE: Mike, being the center of everything, had to bear the burden of helping to craft a script that we could then shoot. Because once you commit, you've got a release date that's driving the train. So there was no turning back.

BAY: It was a very bad way to make a movie. We were stuck in a bad time in Hollywood. And as a director you feel bad because these people are so loyal and they have families. *Transformers* gives 2,000, maybe 2,500 people jobs.

LABEOUF: On that second one, we were in New Mexico, and I'm supposed to stab this spear into Optimus's chest—which is a big blue mound. And there was moisture all over this blue tarp, and I kept slipping. We did one take where I slipped and the spear went into my eye above my retina.

BAY: Oh, I went down to my knees. I thought he lost his eye.

LABEOUF: This liquid started dripping down my face. They thought maybe I had popped my eyeball. I look at Mike, and he drops to his knees and puts his hands over his eyes and starts crying. That's when you know the dude loves you.

BRYCE: I think many of us preferred the heart and soul of the first movie.

KURTZMAN: It was definitely a disappointment for all of us.

LABEOUF: I remember being in London with Mike at the premiere, and I remember coming out of the premiere—and the audience reaction was incredible, actually. It was a really, really solid audience reaction: standing ovation and all that, and we get out, and Mike had this sort of demeanor—he looked fractured.

BAY: You sometimes have to find your way with franchises.

HODENFIELD: Nobody makes a better popcorn movie than Michael Bay. But you're eating that popcorn and drinking your Diet Coke, and after two and a half hours you're gonna have to get up and pee.

JULIE WHITE (ACTOR, *TRANSFORMERS* SERIES): He's just trying to make a fun popcorn movie for you, so? So it's twenty minutes too long. Get over it.

JOSH GREENSTEIN (CO-PRESIDENT, MARKETING, PARAMOUNT): In terms of negative attention, I think that's overblown. The audiences loved the movie. Whether critics did or not, that's another story, but the movie played and ended up grossing over $400 million.

TURTURRO: I thought Two was good. I liked it better than One. A lot of people I know feel that way.

WHITE: After that second movie, I couldn't read anything about it, because the attacks on him seemed so personal. It felt like the critics were all the geeks in high school who had hated the guys who played football or something.

BAY: I did *Transformers: Dark of the Moon* because the studio president came to me, he says: "I'm going to get fucking fired." I really looked him in the eye, and I'm like, "It's a lot of work."

ROB MOORE (VICE CHAIRMAN, PARAMOUNT): That conversation was part of a trip that Adam [Goodman], Michael, and I took to Las Vegas. We were very motivated for him to do the movie and he wasn't sure. What specifically we said? I think there's an expression, *What happens in Vegas, stays in Vegas.* It seems like Michael has broken that rule.

BAY: I'm not going to sit in my house by myself—what am I going to do? Leading the fat cat life—I don't want to do that. I'd rather go back in the trenches.

In Which We Learn There's a Man Inside the Machine

LABEOUF: I've only seen Mike with two women in the six years that I've known him. He wants a family and has the heart for it.

CASE: He's kind of the Warren Beatty of our generation.

ROGER BARTON (EDITOR, VARIOUS BAY FILMS): My wife tries to limit my outings with him.

JON VOIGHT (ACTOR, *PEARL HARBOR, TRANSFORMERS*): He has his girl-friends, all of that stuff. He's an active guy with his gals.

BAY: Well, it was only two [blonds]. But that was two in a row. Normally I don't go out with blonds.

HARRIET BAY: I said, "Oh, Michael, I guess you're going to be like Warren Beatty. He didn't get married until he was fifty." So Michael feels he's got three more years to go.

BAY: It's about finding a wife. I've had a lot of great girlfriends.

WHITE: I just can't see him with somebody over 35.

BAY: I'm a serious guy, but I don't take myself so seriously. Some people are so serious.

GREENSTEIN: That Verizon commercial he did about himself? It's fucking hilarious. That's the real Michael: he is really funny. There's always a little bit of a wink to how he feels about this persona that's out there about him.

WHITE: He is extremely passionate about getting it right and making it cooler. And sometimes—to his own detriment—making it bigger, bigger, bigger!

BAY: They make up words like Bayos and Bayhem and all this crap.

BATES: Through the years, his sentences are getting shorter. Incomplete sentences.

CALVIN WIMMER (EDITOR, *TRANSFORMERS* SERIES): All the words are English, but you have no idea what it is he's talking about. And you gotta go find the people that were nearest around him at that time and try to figure out: "Okay, so this is what he said—what does this mean?" Because it comes so fast.

TURTURRO: Sometimes it's hard because he doesn't always explain himself. His brain is moving so fast.

BARTON: After one of these downloads, I find I need a couple minutes to myself, because I've got a note or a paper full of chicken scratch, which are word fragments because he was talking so fast.

WIMMER: You have to decipher the Bayroglyphics.

JOEL NEGRON (EDITOR, VARIOUS BAY FILMS): I think the recurring editorial theme is: Guess. But guess correctly.

KRUGER: Just when you think he's really upset about something, he'll get off the phone having screamed. He'll throw down the phone and just with a smile, say, "That should get their attention." He's very self-aware.

BAY: The persona comes from . . . I'm a frank guy.

JOHN MALKOVICH (ACTOR, *TRANSFORMERS: Dark of the Moon*): You know, it's an incredible amount of pressure. And sure, somebody could say "He's a junkie for that," or "He likes the authority," but I always think, *God, that must be so lonely.*

BAY: Some nights I sleep like a baby. Other nights it's, *Oh God, I just came up with a bomb shot.*

TYRESE GIBSON (ACTOR, *TRANSFORMERS* SERIES): Sometimes, we'll be hanging out, and Michael just leaves mentally. You can tell, like, he's looking at you, but he's looking through you. His mind is somewhere else. He's thinking about a camera angle, some kind of visual effect.

LABEOUF: Mike is a vulnerable guy. He's the guy who laughs at a joke, then asks you why it's funny.

LAWRENCE: He challenges you to be better, and if you try something and it's not funny or it's not what he's looking for, he will look at you with a blank stare, like, "I don't get it."

SCARLETT JOHANSSON (ACTOR, *THE ISLAND*): I ran into him leaving a party once and asked him if I could be the Easy-Bake Oven Transformer. He looked at me in all seriousness and said, "There isn't one."

In Which the Damsel Calls Our Hero "Hitler"

Before filming began on Transformers: Dark of the Moon, *controversy struck. In an interview with the British magazine* Wonderland, *star Megan Fox said Bay "wants to be like Hitler on his sets, and he is. So he's a nightmare to work for."*

KRUGER: She was there for rehearsals. But she seemed like an actress who didn't want to be a part of it. She was saying she wanted to, but she wasn't acting like it.

BAY: She was in a different world, on her BlackBerry. You gotta stay focused. And you know, the Hitler thing. Steven [Spielberg] said, "Fire her right now."

LABEOUF: Criticism is one thing. Then there's public name-calling, which turns into high school bashing. Which you can't do. She started shit-talking our captain.

BAY: I wasn't hurt, because I know that's just Megan. Megan loves to get a response. And she does it in kind of the wrong way. I'm sorry, Megan. I'm sorry I made you work twelve hours. I'm sorry that I'm making you show up on time. Movies are not always warm and fuzzy. *[Editors note: Fox declined to comment for this article.]*

BRYCE: On the plus side of the column, Rosie has done an enormously wonderful job for being a newcomer.

BAY: Listen, I mean, Rosie came in and she would say hello to the crew. She would acknowledge the crew. She'd say thank you.

ROSIE HUNTINGTON-WHITELEY (MODEL/ACTOR, *TRANSFORMERS: Dark of the Moon*): I was really grateful to everybody, from the people on the catering department to the camera boys to the producers to Shia.

JULIE WHITE (ACTOR, *TRANSFORMER* SERIES): I texted [Megan] and was like, "Come back, Lassie!" Because I think she's magic. She is the *My Little Pony* of *Transformers*.

BAY: She sent me a text three months ago. She said "I hope you're doing well." I responded, "Who is this?" She goes, "Megan, you dork!" I said, "Oh, well, thank you, hope you're well." When you're days and months on a set, it's like a family. You say rude things and you make up. Like, we were shooting a scene in front of the space shuttle and Shia called me a "cocksucker."

LABEOUF: Sometimes to make [a scene] real for me, I need to mindfuck myself. And part of that is having a speaker on set with an iPod plugged in so I can conjure emotions. And some of the songs that I like to play, Mike's not going to have it.

BAY: So Shia's gonna do his emotional scene. He gets out of his car and says, "Michael, you're gonna start with me first." And I said, "No, we're gonna start this way. This is a space shuttle! The United States of America! The last one to be launched!"

LABEOUF: So I'm playing my song and he finally says to me, "No, we're not going to play that song." And he puts on some orchestral *Batman* soundtrack shit. Not for me, you know?

BAY: Then he called me a "cocksucker." But I knew that he had just broken up with his girlfriend. So I didn't go after him. I just said, "That's rude. Don't call me that."

LABEOUF: It was probably the worst argument I've ever had with a co-worker—under a spaceship, screaming at him, "You motherfucker!" All this insanity. Really crazy stuff that I don't feel comfortable repeating, actually. Really gnarly.

BAY: So I ignored him for three days, and that just drives him nuts. "Mike, I'm so sorry! I'm so sorry!" I've had to do a little parenting with Shia, but he's a great kid.

LABEOUF: And then you pull your pants up and you get back to work.

In Which We Learn Our Hero Is, Okay, Yes, a Bit of a Tyrant

JOHANSSON: He can be merciless at times, yet surprisingly sensitive.

SMITH: One day he comes to our trailer and says, "Can you guys step out here for one second?" So we go, and he points up to the sky and says, "You see that big fucking orange thing? When that goes down, this scene's over. So I don't give a fuck what you say—just make sure you say it in my shot."

BRYCE: He is a machine, but he recognizes that he doesn't want to be.

LAWRENCE: I mean, he's like the mad scientist.

BASINGER: And of course, he's a screamer.

FORM: The building shakes.

SMITH: He's a yeller, but he's not really a fighter.

MICHAEL CLARKE DUNCAN (ACTOR, *ARMAGEDDON*): He's like one of those Chihuahuas that's always barking.

LABEOUF: He's got to be a motherfucker. Because there's 90 people marching to the beat of his drum, and there can't be any indecision. And so it's a character that Mike puts on; he's very smart, and you need that guy to make these movies.

TYRESE: He's got this thing in his head, man, he doesn't want to give me too many compliments.

KRUGER: High praise from Michael on an action sequence will be, "That's pretty good."

BATES: If he doesn't eat, he just goes south. If you don't get a peanut butter and jelly sandwich in him, he has a meltdown around lunch hour.

LABEOUF: He's not at all this alpha male, this machismo legend shit— he's not any of these things. You know what he is? New York. If you can make it on a Bay set, you can make it on any set.

HODENFIELD: We all have tried over the years to anticipate what [he wants], but after a certain point you get tired of being told you're dumb.

WALDMAN: He said to me once, "You look familiar. Haven't we met?" I told him I was second unit on *Bad Boys*, and he said, "Oh, I remember you. You sucked."

BATES: He's just a real pain in my ass—and you can write that. I love him like my brother, but I don't talk to my brother. We call him socially retarded sometimes.

HARRIET BAY: I think people would like me to tell horror stories, like he was this devil. But he's really a good kid.

Notes

1. This article appeared on Wired.com on June 26, 2007; https://www.wired.com/2007/06/trans-movie.

2. This article first appeared online at GQ.com on June 27, 2011, http://www.gq.com/story/michael-bay-oral-history.

Feature Films

Bad Boys (1995)
Filming Location: USA
Production: Don Simpson/Jerry Bruckheimer Films
Executive Producers: Lucas Foster, Bruce S. Pustin
Producers: Jerry Bruckheimer, Don Simpson
Distribution: Columbia Pictures
Director: Michael Bay
Story: George Gallo
Screenplay: Michael Barrie, Jim Mulholland, Doug Richardson
Cinematography: Howard Atherton
Music: Mark Mancina
Film Editing: Christian Wagner
Production Design: John Vallone
Costume Design: Bobbie Read
Sound: Peter J. Devlin (production sound mixer), Robert Henderson (supervising sound editor)
Special Effects: Richard Lee Jones (special effects coordinator)
Visual Effects: Kent Demaine (creative director: interactive design)
Production Costs: $19,000,000
Domestic Box Office: $65,800,000
Global Box Office: $141,400,000
Principal Cast: Martin Lawrence (Marcus Burnett), Will Smith (Mike Lowrey), Téa Leoni (Julie Mott), Theresa Randle (Theresa Burnett), Tchéky Karyo (Fouchet), Marg Helgenberger (Alison Sinclair), Joe Pantoliano (Capt. Howard)
Format: 35 mm, color
119 min.

The Rock (1996)
Filming Location: USA

Production: Hollywood Pictures, Don Simpson/Jerry Bruckheimer Films
Executive Producers: Sean Connery, Louis A. Stroller, William Stuart
Producers: Jerry Bruckheimer, Don Simpson
Associate Producers: Kenny Bates, Barry Waldman
Distribution: Buena Vista Pictures
Director: Michael Bay
Story: David Weisberg, Douglas S. Cook
Screenplay: David Weisberg, Douglas S. Cook, Mark Rosner
Cinematography: John Schwartzman
Music: Nick Glennie-Smith, Hans Zimmer
Film Editing: Richard Francis-Bruce
Production Design: Michael White
Costume Design: Bobbie Read
Sound: Robin Haskins (sound recordist), Christopher Boyes (sound designer)
Special Effects: Michael Meinardus (special effects coordinator)
Visual Effects: Rae Griffith (visual effects producer: DQI), Hoyt Yeatman (visual
    effects supervisor)
Production Costs: $75,000,000
Domestic Box Office: $134,000,000
Global Box Office: $335,000,000
Principal Cast: Sean Connery (John Patrick Mason), Nicolas Cage (Stanley
    Goodspeed), Ed Harris (General Francis X. Hummel), Michael Biehn (Com-
    mander Anderson), William Forsythe (Ernest Paxton)
Format: 35 mm, color
136 min.

Armageddon (1998)
Filming Locations: USA, India, France, Turkey, Mexico
Production: Touchstone Pictures, Jerry Bruckheimer Films, Valhalla Motion
    Pictures, Digital Image Associates
Executive Producers: Jonathan Hensleigh, Chad Oman, Jim Van Wyck
Producers: Michael Bay, Jerry Bruckheimer, Gale Ann Hurd
Associate Producers: Kenny Bates, Pat Sandston, Barry Waldman
Distribution: Walt Disney Studios Motion Pictures
Director: Michael Bay
Story: Robert Roy Pool, Jonathan Hensleigh
Screenplay: Jonathan Hensleigh, J. J. Abrams; Tony Gilroy, Shane Salerno (ad-
    aptation)
Cinematography: John Schwartzman
Music: Trevor Rabin
Film Editing: Mark Goldblatt, Chris Lebenzon, Glen Scantlebury
Production Design: Michael White
Costume Design: Magali Guidasci, Michael Kaplan

Sound: Keith A. Wester (production sound mixer), Christopher Boyes (sound designer), George Watters II (supervising sound editor)
Special Effects: John Frazier (special effects supervisor)
Visual Effects: Krystyna Demkowicz (visual effects producer: Matte World), Rae Griffith-Gagnon (visual effects producer: DQI), Josh R. Jaggars (visual effects producer: VIFX), Ken Kokka (visual effects producer: Tippett Studio), Cari Thomas (visual effects producer: Digital Domain), Craig Barron (visual effects supervisor: Matte World), Mark Dornfeld (visual effects supervisor: Buena Vista Imaging), Richard E. Hollander (visual effects supervisor: Blue Sky/VIFX), Richard Hoover (visual effects supervisor), Pat McClung (visual effects supervisor), Erik Nash (visual effects supervisor: Digital Domain), Bruce Nicholson (visual effects supervisor: Tippett Studio), Hoyt Yeatman (visual effects supervisor: Paris destruction sequence: DQI)
Production Costs: $140,000,000
Domestic Box Office: $202,000,000
Global Box Office: $553,700,000
Principal Cast: Bruce Willis (Harry Stamper), Ben Affleck (A. J. Frost), Billy Bob Thornton (Dan Truman), Liv Tyler (Grace Stamper), Will Patton (Chick), Steve Buscemi (Rockhound), Peter Stormare (Lev Andropov), Keith David (General Kimsey)
Format: 35 mm, color
151 min.

Pearl Harbor (2001)
Filming Locations: USA, UK, Mexico
Production: Touchstone Pictures, Jerry Bruckheimer Films
Executive Producers: Scott Gardenhour (executive producer: Baja), Bruce Hendricks, Chad Oman, Mike Stenson, Barry Waldman, Randall Wallace
Producers: Michael Bay, Jerry Bruckheimer
Associate Producers: Kenny Bates, K.C. Hodenfield, Jennifer Klein, Pat Sandston
Line Producer (UK): Selwyn Roberts
Distribution: Walt Disney Studios Motion Pictures
Director: Michael Bay
Screenplay: Randall Wallace
Cinematography: John Schwartzman
Music: Hans Zimmer
Film Editing: Roger Barton, Mark Goldblatt, Chris Lebenzon, Steven Rosenblum
Production Design: Nigel Phelps
Costume Design: Mitzi Haralson, Michael Kaplan
Sound: Peter J. Devlin (production sound mixer), Sean Landeros (sound recordist), Ethan Van der Ryn (sound designer), Christopher Boyes (supervising sound editor), George Watters II (supervising sound editor)

Special Effects: Yves De Bono (special effects supervisor: UK), John Frazier (special effects supervisor), Keith Marbory (special effects supervisor)
Visual Effects: Kathy Chasen-Hay (visual effects producer: Asylum), David S. Dranitzke (visual effects producer: miniatures, ILM), Ned Gorman (visual effects producer: ILM), Jeff Werner (visual effects producer), Eric Brevig (visual effects supervisor), Edward Hirsh (visual effects supervisor), Nathan McGuinness (visual effects supervisor: Asylum)
Production Costs: $140,000,000
Domestic Box Office: $198,500,000
Global Box Office: $449,000,000
Principal Cast: Ben Affleck (Capt. Rafe McCawley), Josh Hartnett (Capt. Danny Walker), Kate Beckinsale (Nurse Lt. Evelyn Johnson), Cuba Gooding Jr. (Petty Officer Doris Miller), Tom Sizemore (Sgt. Earl Sistern), Jon Voight (President Franklin Delano Roosevelt), Colm Feore (Adm. Husband E. Kimmel), Alec Baldwin (Lt. Col. James Doolittle)
Format: 35 mm, color, black-and-white (archive footage)
183 min.

Bad Boys II (2003)
Filming Locations: USA, Puerto Rico, Netherlands
Production: Columbia Pictures, Don Simpson/Jerry Bruckheimer Films
Executive Producers: Chad Oman, Mike Stenson, Barry Waldman
Producer: Jerry Bruckheimer
Associate Producers: Matthew Cohan, Don Ferrarone, Pat Sandston
Distribution: Columbia Pictures
Director: Michael Bay
Story: Marianne Wibberley, Cormac Wibberley, Ron Shelton, based on characters by George Gallo
Screenplay: Ron Shelton and Jerry Stahl
Cinematography: Amir Mokri
Music: Trevor Rabin
Film Editing: Roger Barton, Mark Goldblatt, Thomas A. Muldoon
Production Design: Dominic Watkins
Costume Design: Carol Ramsey, Deborah L. Scott
Sound: Peter J. Devlin (sound mixer), George Watters II (supervising sound editor)
Special Effects: John Frazier (special effects supervisor)
Visual Effects: Blondel Aidoo (executive visual effects producer: Asylum), Ladd Lanford (visual effects producer: Pacific Title), Jamie Stevenson (visual effects producer: Asylum), David Taritero (visual effects producer), Mark Freund (visual effects supervisor: Pacific Title), David Jones (visual effects supervisor: Asylum), Rob Legato (visual effects supervisor), Nathan McGuinness (senior visual effects supervisor: Asylum), Carey Villegas (visual effects supervisor)

Production Costs: $130,000,000
Domestic Box Office: $138,600,000
Global Box Office: $273,000,000
Principal Cast: Martin Lawrence (Marcus Burnett), Will Smith (Mike Lowrey), Jordi Mollà (Hector Juan Carlos "Johnny" Tapia), Gabrielle Union (Syd), Peter Stormare (Alexei), Theresa Randle (Theresa), Joe Pantoliano (Captain Howard)
Format: 35 mm, color
147 min.

The Island (2005)
Filming Location: USA
Production: DreamWorks SKG, Warner Bros., Parkes+MacDonald Image Nation
Executive Producer: Laurie MacDonald
Producers: Michael Bay, Ian Bryce, Walter F. Parkes
Associate Producers: Ken Bates, Matthew Cohan, Heidi Fugeman Lindelof, Josh McLaglen, Steven P. Saeta
Distribution: DreamWorks Pictures (USA), Warner Bros. Pictures (international)
Director: Michael Bay
Story: Caspian Tredwell-Owen
Screenplay: Caspian Tredwell-Owen, and Alex Kurtzman, Roberto Orci
Cinematography: Mauro Fiore
Music: Steve Jablonsky
Film Editing: Paul Rubell, Christian Wagner
Production Design: Nigel Phelps
Costume Design: Deborah L. Scott
Sound: Maurizio Argentieri (sound mixer: Italy), Peter J. Devlin (sound mixer), Karen Baker Landers (supervising sound editor), Per Hallberg (supervising sound editor)
Special Effects: Michael Deak (special effects supervisor)
Visual Effects: Kimberly Covate (visual effects producer: Asylum), Shari Hanson (visual effects producer), Eric Brevig (visual effects supervisor), Nathan McGuinness (senior visual effects supervisor: Asylum), Will Robbins (visual effects supervisor: Black Box Digital), Marc Varisco (visual effects supervisor: Asylum)
Production Costs: $126,000,000
Domestic Box Office: $36,000,000
Global Box Office: $163,000,000
Principal Cast: Ewan McGregor (Lincoln Six Echo/Tom Lincoln), Scarlett Johansson (Jordan Two Delta/Sarah Jordan), Djimon Hounsou (Albert Laurent), Sean Bean (Dr. Bernard Merrick), Michael Clarke Duncan (Starkweather Two Delta/Jamal Starkweather), Steve Buscemi (James McCord)

Format: 35 mm, color
136 min.

Transformers (2007)
Filming Location: USA
Production: DreamWorks SKG, Paramount Pictures, Hasbro, di Bonaventura
    Pictures, Amblin Entertainment, Platinum Dunes, SprocketHeads, think-
    film
Executive Producers: Michael Bay, Brian Goldner, Steven Spielberg, Mark
    Vahradian
Producers: Ian Bryce, Tom DeSanto, Lorenzo di Bonaventura, Don Murphy
Associate Producers: Matthew Cohan, Michelle McGonagle
Co-Producers: Ken Bates, Allegra Clegg
Transmedia Producer: George Strayton
Producer, IMAX Version: Lorne Orleans
Distribution: DreamWorks Pictures (USA), Paramount Pictures (international)
Director: Michael Bay
Story: John Rogers, Roberto Orci, Alex Kurtzman
Screenplay: Roberto Orci, Alex Kurtzman
Cinematography: Mitchell Amundsen
Music: Steve Jablonsky
Film Editing: Thomas A. Muldoon, Paul Rubell, Glen Scantlebury
Production Design: Jeff Mann
Costume Design: Deborah L. Scott
Sound: Peter J. Devlin (sound mixer), Kevin O'Connell (sound mixer), Erik
    Aadahl (sound designer), Mike Hopkins (supervising sound editor), Ethan
    Van der Ryn (supervising sound editor)
Special Effects: John Frazier (special effects supervisor), Geoff Heron (minia-
    ture special effects supervisor: Kerner Optical)
Visual Effects: Kathy Chasen-Hay (visual effects producer: Asylum), Shari Han-
    son (visual effects producer), Tim Jacobsen (visual effects producer), David
    James (visual effects producer: Digital Domain), Scott Farrar (visual effects
    supervisor: ILM), Richard Kidd (visual effects supervisor), Nathan McGuin-
    ness (senior visual effects supervisor: Asylum), David Prescott (visual effects
    supervisor: Digital Domain)
Production Costs: $150,000,000
Domestic Box Office: $319,000,000
Global Box Office: $709,700,000
Principal Cast: Shia LaBeouf (Sam Witwicky), Tyrese Gibson (USAF Tech Ser-
    geant Epps), Josh Duhamel (Captain William Lennox), Anthony Anderson
    (Glen Whitmann), Megan Fox (Mikaela Banes), Rachael Taylor (Maggie
    Madsen), John Turturro (Agent Simmons), Jon Voight (Defense Secretary
    John Keller)

Format: 35 mm/70 mm (IMAX), color
144 min.

Transformers: Revenge of the Fallen (2009)
Filming Locations: USA, Jordan, Egypt, China, France
Production: DreamWorks Pictures, Paramount Pictures, Hasbro, di Bonaventura
    Pictures, Amblin Entertainment, Platinum Dunes
Executive Producers: Michael Bay, Brian Goldner, Steven Spielberg, Mark
    Vahradian
Producers: Ian Bryce, Tom DeSanto, Lorenzo di Bonaventura, Don Murphy
Associate Producers: Matthew Cohan, K.C. Hodenfield, Michelle McGonagle
Co-Producers: Ken Bates, Allegra Clegg
Production Executive: David Ready
Distribution: DreamWorks Pictures, Paramount Pictures
Director: Michael Bay
Screenplay: Ehren Kruger, Roberto Orci, Alex Kurtzman
Cinematography: Ben Seresin
Music: Steve Jablonsky
Film Editing: Roger Barton, Thomas A. Muldoon, Joel Negron, Paul Rubell
Production Design: Nigel Phelps
Costume Design: Deborah L. Scott
Sound: Geoffrey Patterson (sound mixer), Erik Aadahl (supervising sound edi-
    tor), Ethan Van der Ryn (supervising sound editor)
Special Effects: John Frazier (special effects supervisor), Wayne Toth (special
    effects supervisor: KNB Effects Group)
Visual Effects: Wayne Billheimer (visual effects producer), Elizabeth Hitt (vi-
    sual effects producer), Julian Levi (visual effects producer: Digital Domain),
    Shreyas Patil (background prep lead; West Wing Digital Studio), Raena Singh
    (visual effects producer: Catalyst Media), Dereck Sonnenburg (visual effects
    producer), Matthew E. Butler (visual effects supervisor: Digital Domain),
    Scott Farrar (visual effects supervisor), Richard Kidd (visual effects supervi-
    sor), Nathan McGuinness (senior visual effects supervisor: Asylum)
Production Costs: $200,000,000
Domestic Box Office: $402,000,000
Global Box Office: $836,300,000
Principal Cast: Shia LaBeouf (Sam Witwicky), Megan Fox (Mikaela Banes),
    Josh Duhamel (Major Lennox), Tyrese Gibson (USAF Chief Master Sergeant
    Epps), John Turturro (Simmons), Peter Cullen (Optimus Prime—voice)
Format: 35 mm/70 mm (IMAX)/D-Cinema (3-D), color
150 min.

Transformers: Dark of the Moon (2011)
Filming Locations: USA, Russia, Cambodia

Production: Paramount Pictures, Hasbro, di Bonaventura Pictures, Amblin
Entertainment, Platinum Dunes
Executive Producers: Michael Bay, Brian Goldner, Steven Spielberg, Mark
Vahradian
Producers: Ian Bryce, Tom Desanto, Lorenzo di Bonaventura, Don Murphy
Associate Producers: Matthew Cohan, Michael Kase
Co-Producers: Ken Bates, Allegra Clegg
Distribution: Paramount Pictures
Director: Michael Bay
Screenplay: Ehren Kruger
Cinematography: Amir Mokri
Music: Steve Jablonsky
Film Editing: Roger Barton, William Goldenberg, Joel Negron
Production Design: Nigel Phelps
Costume Design: Deborah L. Scott
Sound: Peter J. Devlin (sound mixer), Erik Aadahl (supervising sound editor),
Ethan Van Der Ryn (supervising sound editor)
Special Effects: John Frazier (special effects supervisor), John D. Milinac (spe-
cial effects supervisor: Chicago)
Visual Effects: Wayne Billheimer (visual effects producer: ILM), Michelle Winze
(visual effects producer: Digital Domain), Tony Baldridge (visual effects su-
pervisor: Legend 3D), Matthew Butler (visual effects supervisor: Digital Do-
main), Brennan Doyle (visual effects supervisor: Singapore, Industrial Light
& Magic), Scott Farrar (visual effects supervisor), Mike Miller (stereoscopic
visual effects supervisor: In-Three), Scott Squires (senior visual effects su-
pervisor: Legend 3D), Jeff White (co-visual effects supervisor: Industrial
Light & Magic)
Production Costs: $195,000,000
Domestic Box Office: $352,400,000
Global Box Office: $1,124,000,000
Principal Cast: Shia LaBeouf (Sam Witwicky), Josh Duhamel (Lennox), John Tur-
turro (Simmons), Tyrese Gibson (Epps), Rosie Huntington-Whiteley (Carly),
Patrick Dempsey (Dylan), Kevin Dunn (Ron Witwicky), Julie White (Judy
Witwicky), John Malkovich (Bruce Brazos), Frances McDormand (Mearing)
Format: 35 mm/70 mm (IMAX)/D-Cinema (3-D), color
154 min.

Pain & Gain (2013)
Filming Location: USA
Production: Paramount Pictures, De Line Pictures
Executive Producers: Matthew Cohan, Scott Gardenhour, Wendy Japhet
Producers: Michael Bay, Ian Bryce, Donald De Line
Co-Producers: Michael Kase, Alma Kuttruff

Distribution: Paramount Pictures
Director: Michael Bay
Screenplay: Christopher Markus and Stephen McFeely, based on the magazine
articles by Pete Collins
Cinematography: Ben Seresin
Music: Steve Jablonsky
Film Editing: Thomas A. Muldoon, Joel Negron
Production Design: Jeffrey Beecroft
Costume Design: Deborah L. Scott, Colleen Kelsall (co-costume designer)
Sound: David Husby (production sound mixer), Erik Aadahl (sound designer),
Ethan Van der Ryn (sound designer)
Special Effects: John Frazier (special effects supervisor)
Visual Effects: Pablo Helman (visual effects supervisor: ILM), Nancy Lamon-
tagne (visual effects coordinator: Rodeo FX)
Production Costs: $26,000,000
Domestic Box Office: $50,000,000
Global Box Office: $86,000,000
Principal Cast: Mark Wahlberg (Daniel Lugo), Dwayne Johnson (Paul Doyle),
Anthony Mackie (Adrian Doorbal), Tony Shalhoub (Victor Kershaw), Ed
Harris (Ed DuBois)
Format: 35 mm/D-Cinema (3-D), color
129 min.

Transformers: Age of Extinction (2014)
Filming Locations: China, USA, Iceland
Production: Paramount Pictures, Hasbro, di Bonaventura Pictures, Tom De-
Santo/Don Murphy Production, Ian Bryce Productions, Amblin Entertain-
ment, China Movie Channel, Platinum Dunes
Executive Producers: Michael Bay, Brian Goldner, Steven Spielberg, Mark
Vahradian
Producers: Ian Bryce, Tom DeSanto, Lorenzo di Bonaventura, Don Murphy
Associate Producer: Regan Riskas
Co-Producers: Allegra Clegg, Matthew Cohan, Brian Goldner, K.C. Hodenfield,
Michael Kase, Dany Wolf (co-producer: Wulong)
Line Producer (China, pre-production): Chiu Wah Lee
Distribution: Paramount Pictures
Director: Michael Bay
Screenplay: Ehren Kruger
Cinematography: Amir Mokri
Music: Steve Jablonsky
Film Editing: Roger Barton, William Goldenberg, Paul Rubell
Production Design: Jeffrey Beecroft
Costume Design: Marie-Sylvie Deveau

Sound: Peter J. Devlin (sound mixer), Clayton Perry (sound mixer), Erik Aadahl (sound designer), John Marquis (sound designer), Tobias Poppe (sound designer), Ethan Van der Ryn (sound designer)

Special Effects: John Frazier (special effects supervisor)

Visual Effects: Greg Maloney (visual effects producer: 32Ten Studios), Karey Maltzahn (visual effects producer), Abhishek More (senior visual effects producer: Digikore), Jinnie Pak (visual effects producer: method studios), Ben Pickering (visual effects producer), Shelly Sharma (visual effects producer: Alien Sense), Dane Allan Smith (visual effects producer: Digikore), Mark Van Ee (visual effects producer), Kevin Baillie (visual effects supervisor: Atomic Fiction), Ahdee Chiu (visual effects supervisor), Nigel Denton-Howes (visual effects supervisor: Prime Focus), Scott Farrar (visual effects supervisor: ILM), Mohen Leo (visual effects supervisor: ILM Singapore), Ollie Rankin (visual effects supervisor: method studios), Greg Steele (visual effects supervisor (Method Studios), Pat Tubach (co-visual effects supervisor: ILM), Jeff White (visual effects supervisor)

Production Costs: $210,000,000

Domestic Box Office: $245,400,000

Global Box Office: $1,104,000,000

Principal Cast: Mark Wahlberg (Cade Yeager), Stanley Tucci (Joshua Joyce), Kelsey Grammer (Harold Attinger), Peter Cullen (Optimus Prime—voice)

Format: 35 mm/D-Cinema (3-D), color

165 min.

13 Hours: The Secret Soldiers of Benghazi (2016)

Filming Locations: Malta, Morocco

Production: 3 Arts Entertainment, Bay Films, Dune Films, Latina Pictures, Paramount Pictures

Executive Producers: Richard Abate, Matthew Cohan, Scott Gardenhour

Producers: Michael Bay, Erwin Stoff

Associate Producer: Harry Humphries

Co-Producers: Ken Bates, Michael Kase

Line Producer (Morocco): Jimmy Abounouom

Distribution: Paramount Pictures

Director: Michael Bay

Screenplay: Chuck Hogan, based on the book by Mitchell Zuckoff

Cinematography: Dion Beebe

Music: Lorne Balfe

Film Editing: Michael McCusker, Pietro Scalia, Calvin Wimmer

Production Design: Jeffrey Beecroft

Costume Design: Deborah Lynn Scott

Sound: Mac Ruth (production sound mixer), Matt Cavanaugh (sound recordist), Brandon Jones (sound designer), Tobias Poppe (sound designer), Tim

Walston (sound designer), Erik Aadahl (supervising sound editor), Ethan Van der Ryn (supervising sound editor)

Special Effects: Kenneth Cassar (special effects supervisor: Malta), Terry Glass (special effects supervisor)

Visual Effects: Wayne Billheimer (visual effects producer: ILM), Scott Farrar (visual effects supervisor: ILM), Varun Hakdar (visual effects supervisor: BaseFX)

Production Costs: $50,000,000

Domestic Box Office: $53,000,000

Global Box Office: $69,400,000

Principal Cast: James Badge Dale (Tyrone "Rone" Woods), John Krasinski (Jack Silva), Max Martini (Mark "Oz" Geist), Pablo Schreiber (Kris "Tanto" Paronto), Toby Stephens (Glen "Bub" Doherty)

Format: 35 mm/D-Cinema (3-D), color

144 min.

Transformers: The Last Knight (2017)

Filming Locations: Cuba, England (UK), Northern Ireland (UK), Norway, Scotland (UK), USA

Production: Di Bonaventura Pictures, Hasbro Studios

Executive Producer: Michael Bay, Brian Goldner, Steven Spielberg, Mark Vahradian

Producers: Ian Bryce, Tom DeSanto, Lorenzo di Bonaventura, Don Murphy

Co-Producers: Matthew Cohan, Michael Kase, Ricardo del Río (Cuba)

Line Producer (Cuba): Arturo del Río

Distribution: Paramount Pictures

Director: Michael Bay

Screenplay: Art Marcum, Matt Holloway, Ken Nolan; based on the story by Akiva Goldsman, Art Marcum, Matt Holloway, and Ken Nolan

Cinematography: Jonathan Sela

Music: Steve Jablonsky

Film Editing: Roger Barton, Adam Gerstel, John Refoua, Mark Sanger

Sound: Erik Aadahl (sound designer), Ethan Van der Ryn (supervising sound editor)

Special Effects: John Frazier (special effects supervisor), Terry Glass (UK special effects supervisor)

Visual Effects: Ryan Church (vfx art director: ILM), Scott Farrar (visual effects supervisor), Julian Foddy (visual effects supervisor: ILM), George Kolyras (visual effects coordinator), Rick Lupton (vfx supervisor: iSolve Inc.), Bonita Nichols (visual effects coordinator), Bryan Ryan (visual effects coordinator: MPC), Marc Sadeghi (executive visual effects producer: atomic fiction), Craig Saxby (visual effects coordinator: mpc), Brian Sepanzyk (visual effects coordinator: ILM), Jason Smith (visual effects supervisor), Kath Smith (visual effects coordinator), Ryan Wiederkehr (visual effects producer: ILM)

Production Costs: $260,000,000
Principal Cast: Mark Wahlberg (Cade Yeager), Stanley Tucci (Joshua Joyce), Isabela Moner (Izabella), Josh Duhamel (Lt. Col. William Lennox), John Turturro (Agent Simmons), Anthony Hopkins (Sir Edmund Burton)
Format: D-Cinema (3-D), color

Music Videos, Documentaries, Commercials (selection)

"I Love You" (1990)
Music Video for Vanilla Ice
Director: Michael Bay

"I Touch Myself" (1990)
Music Video for the Divinyls
Director: Michael Bay

Playboy: Kerri Kendall—September 1990 Video Centerfold (1990)
Documentary for *Playboy*
Director: Michael Bay

"Do It to Me" (1992)
Music Video for Lionel Richie
Director: Michael Bay

"You Won't See Me Cry" (1992)
Music Video for Wilson Phillips
Director: Michael Bay

"I'd Do Anything for Love (But I Won't Do That)" (1993)
Music Video for Meatloaf
Director: Michael Bay

"Aaron Burr" (1994)
Commercial for California Milk
Director: Michael Bay

"Lawyer Roundup" (1994)
Commercial for Miller Lite
Director: Michael Bay

"Jordan vs. Barkley" (1994)
Commercial for Nike
Director: Michael Bay

Films Produced

Armageddon (1998) — Producer
Pearl Harbor (2001) — Producer
The Texas Chainsaw Massacre (2003) — Producer
The Amityville Horror (2005) — Producer
The Island (2005) — Producer
In the Blink of an Eye (2005) — Consulting producer
The Texas Chainsaw Massacre: The Beginning (2006) — Producer
From Script to Sand: The Skorponok Desert Attack (2007) — Executive producer
The Hitcher (2007) — Producer
Transformers (2007) — Executive producer
Our World (2007) — Executive producer
Their War (2007) — Producer
The Unborn (2009) — Producer
Horsemen (2009) — Producer
Friday the 13th (2009) — Producer
Transformers: Revenge of the Fallen (2009) — Executive producer
A Nightmare on Elm Street (2010) — Producer
I Am Number Four (2011) — Producer
Transformers: Dark of the Moon (2011) — Executive producer
Above and Beyond: Exploring Dark of the Moon (2012) — Executive producer
Uncharted Territory: NASA's Future Then and Now (2012) — Executive producer
Occult (2013) — TV movie; Executive producer
Pain & Gain: The A Game—Michael Bay's 'Pain & Gain' (2013) — Executive producer
Pain & Gain (2013) — Producer
The Purge (2013) — Producer
Ouija (2014) — Producer
Teenage Mutant Ninja Turtles (2014) — Producer
The Purge: Anarchy (2014) — Producer
Transformers: Age of Extinction (2014) — Executive producer
The Last Ship (2014–2016) — TV series; Executive producer
Black Sails (2014–2015) — TV series; Executive producer
Project Almanac (2015) — Producer
Teenage Mutant Ninja Turtles: Out of the Shadows (2016) — Producer
Billion Dollar Wreck (2016) — TV series; Executive producer
13 Hours (2016) — Producer
The Purge: Election Year (2016) — Producer
Transformers: The Last Knight (2017) — Executive producer

On Michael Bay

Baker, Brian. "The Cinema Within: Spectacle, Labour, and Utopia in Michael Bay's *The Island*." *Senses of Cinema* 75 (2015).

Bennett, Bruce. "The Cinema of Michael Bay: An Aesthetic of Excess." *Senses of Cinema* 75 (2015).

Bennett, Bruce, Leon Gurevitch, and Bruce Isaacs. "The Cinema of Michael Bay: Technology, Transformation, and Spectacle in the 'Post-Cinematic' Era." *Senses of Cinema* 75 (2015).

Every Frame a Painting. "Michael Bay—What Is Bayhem?" Online video clip. *YouTube*. July 3, 2014.

Geraghty, Lincoln. "Authenticity, Popular Aesthetics, and the Subcultural Politics of an Unwanted Blockbuster: The Case of Transformers." *Valuing Films: Shifting Perceptions of Worth*. Edited by Laura Hubner. Basingstoke: Palgrave Macmillan, 2011. 88–105.

Gurevitch, Leon. "The Transforming Face of Industrial Spectacle: A Media Archaeology of Machinic Mobility." *Senses of Cinema* 75 (2015).

ILMVisualFX. "Behind the Magic: The Visual Effects of 'Transformers Age of Extinction.'" Online video clip. *YouTube*. December 18, 2014.

Isaacs, Bruce. "The Mechanics of Continuity in Michael Bay's *Transformers* Franchise." *Senses of Cinema* 75 (2015).

Lee, Kevin B. "Transformers: The Premake." Online videodocumentary. *YouTube*. June 27, 2014.

Purse, Linda. "Rotational Aesthetics: Michael Bay and Contemporary Cinema's Machine Movement." *Senses of Cinema* 75 (2015).

Shook, John R., and Liz Stillwaggon Swan, eds. *Transformers and Philosophy: More Than Meets the Mind*. Chicago: Open Court, 2009.

Stork, Matthias. "Chaos Cinema Part 1." Online video clip. *Vimeo*. August 22, 2011. https://vimeo.com/28016047.

———. "Chaos Cinema Part 3." Online video clip. *Vimeo*. 2012. https://vimeo.com/40881319.

Whalley, Jim. "'A process to learn something': *Pearl Harbor* and the Producer's Game in Contemporary Hollywood." *New Review of Film and Television Studies* 9, no. 3 (2011): 265–82.

Wilson, D. Harlan. "Technomasculine Bodies and Vehicles of Desire: The Erotic Delirium of Michael Bay's *Transformers*." *Extrapolation* 53, no. 3 (2012): 347–64.

Related Books and Essays

Bather, Neil. "Big Rocks, Big Bangs, Big Bucks: The Spectacle of Evil in the Popular Cinema of Jerry Bruckheimer." *New Review of Film and Television Studies* 2, no. 1 (2004): 37–59.

Bordwell, David. "Intensified Continuity: Visual Style in Contemporary American Film." *Film Quarterly* 55, no. 3 (2002): 16–28.

Calavita, Marco. "'MTV Aesthetics' at the Movies: Interrogating a Film Criticism Fallacy." *Journal of Film and Video* 59, no. 3 (2007): 15–31.

CineFix. "6 Reasons You have to respect Michael Bay!!!!!!!!!!!!!!!!—Film School'D." Online video clip. *YouTube*. September 23, 2015.

Clover, Joshua. "Dream Machines." *Film Quarterly* 61, no. 2 (2007): 6–7.

Curtis, Bryan. "The Bad Boy of Summer." *Slate*. June 15, 2005.

Diamond, Jamie. "One Director Who's Proud to Be Called Commercial." *New York Times*. June 16, 1996.

Gurevitch, Leon. "The Cinemas of Interactions: Cinematics and the 'Game Effect' in the Age of Digital Attractions." *Senses of Cinema* 57 (2010).

Handlen, Zack. "Bay-watch: The Hunt for Meaning in the Films of Michael Bay." *A.V. Club*. August 21, 2009.

Itzkoff, Dave. "Putting Away His Toys." *New York Times*. April 17, 2013.

Jones, Kent. "Bay Watch." *Film Comment* 37, no. 4 (2001): 27–29.

Murray, Noel. "I Watched This on Purpose: *Transformers* and *Transformers: Revenge of the Fallen*." *A.V. Club*. February 10, 2010.

Palmer, Lorrie. "'Cranked' Masculinity: Hypermediation in Digital Action Cinema." *Cinema Journal* 51, no. 4 (2012): 1–25.

Phipps, Keith. "I Watched This on Purpose: *The Island*." *A.V. Club*. April 8, 2009.

Purse, Lisa. "Affective Trajectories: Locating Diegetic Velocity in the Cinema Experience." *Cinema Journal* 55, no. 2 (2016): 151–57.

Rabin, Nathan. "I Watched This on Purpose: *Bad Boys*." *A.V. Club*. July 15, 2009.

Seitz, Matt Zoller. "Directors of the Decade: No. 10 Michael Bay." *Salon*. December 16, 2009.

Semley, John. "Michael Bay Brings Scorched-Earth Politics to the Big Screen." *Maclean's*. January 16, 2016.

Smith, Gavin. "Movies That Mattered: For Better or for Worse." *Film Comment* 46, no. 1 (2010): 46–48.

White, Geoffrey M. "Disney's *Pearl Harbor*: National Memory at the Movies." *Public Historian* 24, no. 4 (2002): 97–115.

Lutz Koepnick is Gertrude Conaway Vanderbilt Professor of German, Cinema and Media Arts at Vanderbilt University, where he also chairs the Department of German, Russian, and East European Studies and directs the joint PhD program in Comparative Media Analysis and Practice. His books include *On Slowness: Toward an Aesthetic of the Contemporary* and *The Dark Mirror: German Cinema between Hitler and Hollywood*.

Books in the series Contemporary Film Directors

Richard Linklater
David T. Johnson

David Lynch
Justus Nieland

John Sayles
David R. Shumway

Dario Argento
L. Andrew Cooper

Todd Haynes
Rob White

Christian Petzold
Jaimey Fisher

Spike Lee
Todd McGowan

Terence Davies
Michael Koresky

Francis Ford Coppola
Jeff Menne

Emir Kusturica
Giorgio Bertellini

Agnès Varda
Kelley Conway

John Lasseter
Richard Neupert

Paul Thomas Anderson
George Toles

Cristi Puiu
Monica Filimon

Wes Anderson
Donna Kornhaber

Jan Švankmajer
Keith Leslie Johnson

Kelly Reichardt
Katherine Fusco and Nicole Seymour

Michael Bay
Lutz Koepnick

The University of Illinois Press
is a founding member of the
Association of American University Presses.

University of Illinois Press
1325 South Oak Street
Champaign, IL 61820-6903
www.press.uillinois.edu